HANA GAJDOŠTÍKOVÁ

Czech National Cookbook

Hana Gajdoštíková
Czech National Cookbook

Photography: Viktor Kronbauer
Cover and graphic design: Vladimír Nárožník
Layout: MU Typographic Studio
Printed by Ekon, Jihlava
Published by Jan Kanzelsberger Publishing House,
Václavské nám. 42, 110 00 Prague
1st edition, Prague: 5000

ISBN 80-85387-36-0

Meat Dishes

Fish

Fowl and Game

Meatless Dishes

Assorted Dumplings

Fancy Desserts, Cakes and Holiday Treats

Measures

In this edition all weights and liquid measures are given in metric and imperial. A teaspoon (tsp.) refers to a 5ml spoon and a tablespoon (Tbsp.) to a 15ml spoon. Because the equivalents are only approximate either metric or imperial should be used throughout each recipe.

Liquid Measures	Solid Measures
150 ml = 1/4 pint	25 g = 1 oz
300 ml = 1/2 pint	225–250 g = 8 oz
1/2 l = 1 pint	450–500 g = 16 oz or 1 lb.

Soups

Cream of Chicken Soup (Kaldoun)

Chicken, duck or goose giblets 500 g (16 oz), root vegetables (carrots, parsnips, celeriac, etc.), 1 onion, 50 g (2 oz) butter, 60 g (2 1/4 oz) flour, 2–3 whole peppercorns, salt, nutmeg, 1 cube chicken bouillon, chopped parsley.

Cover giblets with water, add salt, cleaned root vegetables, onion and whole peppercorns. Cook till meat is tender. Strain soup, and chop giblets. Melt butter in pan, stir in flour and cook until golden. Add to soup pot, add chopped giblets and cook 15 more minutes. Add bouillon and a dash of nutmeg. Sprinkle with chopped parsley before serving. You can also add breadcrumb dumplings.

Breadcrumb Dumplings

1 tsp. butter, 1 egg, 3 Tbs. breadcrumbs, 3 Tbs. milk, salt, nutmeg, and chopped parsley.

Mix eggs and butter together till smooth. Soak breadcrumbs with milk, add to egg mixture, and pinch of salt, dash of nutmeg and chopped parsley. Mix well, form mixture into small balls, drop in boiling soup and cook 5–10 minutes or till dumplings are done.

Fish Soup (Czech Christmas Soup)

Head and tail pieces of hen carp, fish roe, 2–3 fillets, root vegetables, 2 onions, 50 g (2 oz) butter, 60 g (2 1/4 oz) flour, salt, pepper, nutmeg, chopped parsley.

Sauté fine chopped root vegetables, onion and fish roe in 1 Tbsp. butter. Cook fish head, tail and fillets in salted water with 1 onion till soft. Strain soup, add broth to sautéd vegetables. Brown rest of butter with flour, add broth and cook 30 minutes. Remove fish from bones, add to soup, salt, pepper and nutmeg to taste. Before serving add chopped parsley and buttered croutons.

Tripe Soup

1 1/2 kg (3 lbs) fresh tripe, root vegetables (carrots, parsnip, celeriac),
2 onions, 80 g (3 oz) butter, 100 g (4 oz) flour, salt, 2 bouillon cubes,
marjoram, garlic, pepper, sweet & hot paprika, 1 tsp. lard, chopped parsley.

Wash tripe in boiling water and clean well. Simmer in water
30 minutes and strain. Add hot water to tripe again, add salt
and onion and cook at least 3 hours, until tender, add root
vegetables for last half-hour. Strain broth and cut tripe into
narrow strips. Melt butter, add flour and finely chopped
onion, cook until golden in color, and add to broth with cut
tripe and 2 bouillon cubes, cook for 20 minutes. Add
paprika, pepper, marjoram, and parsley and crushed garlic
on melted lard.

Potato Soup

3 large potatoes, 1 1/2 l (3 pints) water, root vegetables, 1 onion, fresh or
dried mushrooms (Soak dried mushrooms for 1 hour before using),
60 g (2 1/4 oz) butter, salt, marjoram, caraway seed, garlic and chopped
parsley.

Sauté finely chopped root vegetables, onion and mushrooms
in butter, sprinkle with flour, add part of water and mix well.
Add rest of water, diced potatoes and caraway seed. Salt to
taste and cook till tender. When finished add marjoram,
crushed garlic and chopped parley.

Mushroom Soup with Veal Sweetbreads

400 g (14 oz) beef, root vegetables, 250 g (8 oz) veal sweetbreads, salt,
1 bouillon cube, 1 onion, 30 g (1 1/4 oz) butter, 250 g (8 oz) fresh
mushrooms, and chopped parsley.

Simmer beef and root vegetables in 3 pints salted water until
tender. Meanwhile wash sweetbreads and put in boiling
salted water for 2–3 minutes, remove membranes. In last

20 minutes of cooking add sweetbreads to beef. Sauté finely chopped onion and mushrooms in butter with chopped parsley. Strain soup, dice sweetbreads. Boiled beef can be used with a sauce or vegetables as a main course.

Beef Soup with Liver Dumplings

400 g (14 oz) beef (Chuck or Rump), 1 1/2 l (3pints) water, root vegetables (carrot, parsnip, celeriac, onion).

Wash meat and add cold salted water, root vegetables and cook slowly until tender, about 2 hours. Strain, finely dice beef, add to broth with liver dumplings, cook 5 more minutes or until liver dumplings are done. Sprinkle with chopped parsley.

Liver Dumplings

100 g (4 oz) Veal or Beef Liver, l egg, butter 1oz, 3 Tbsp bread crumbs, 3 Tbsp broth, salt, pepper, 1 clove garlic.

Mix butter with egg, add pinch salt, dash pepper and crushed clove of garlic. Mix breadcrumbs with broth. Scrape liver on a board, make sure all veins and membranes are removed. Mix all ingredients, stand for 2–3 minutes. Form small dumplings, drop into soup, simmer 5 minutes or until dumplings are done.

Sauerkraut Soup

200 g (7 oz) Sauerkraut, 11/4 l (2 1/2 pints) water, 2 potatoes, 2 Tbsp. flour, 1 onion, 40 g (1 1/2 oz) bacon, 100 g (4 oz) Polish beef sausage, salt, caraway seed, sweet paprika, 4 Tbsp. sour cream.

Sauté finely diced bacon. Add sliced Polish sausage and finely chopped onion. Sprinkle with flour. Add water, salt and cook until tender. When finished mix in sour cream.

Potato Soup with Meat Dumplings

1 Tbsp. oil, 1 Tbsp. chopped onion, 1 clove of garlic diced, 1/2 l (1 pint) water, 1 tsp. salt, 1 1/4 kg (2 1/2 lbs.) finely diced potatoes, 2 Tbsp. oil, 100 g (4 oz) bacon, root vegetables, 300 g (11 oz) red and green bell pepper, 1 1/2 l chicken stock (3 pints).

Sauté onion and garlic in oil. Add water, potatoes and salt, cook until tender. Press cooked potatoes through sieve, add stock. Sauté bacon in oil. Add finely diced root vegetables and bell peppers. Simmer 10 minutes and add to soup.

Meat Dumplings

200 g (7 oz) Ground beef and pork, 30 g (1 1/4 oz) bread crumbs, 1 grated onion, 1 egg, 1 Tbsp. grated cheese, salt, pepper and paprika.

Mix all ingredients. Form small dumplings, add to boiling soup and simmer until dumplings are done, about 10–15 minutes.

Garlic Croutons

2 rolls diced, 1 Tbsp. butter, 1 clove garlic crushed.

Sauté diced rolls in hot butter with garlic, add to soup before serving.

Garlic Soup

1 l (2 pints) water, 40 g (1 1/4 oz) lard, salt, 4 cloves garlic, pepper, marjoram, caraway seeds, chives, 2 slices toasted rye bread.

To salted boiling water add lard, caraway seed and crushed garlic. Simmer. Add pepper and marjoram. Place toasted bread in each soup bowl, add soup and sprinkle with chopped chives.

Bouillon with Lardon Dumplings

3 onions, root vegetables, 1 Tbsp. oil, 500 g (1lb) beef bones,
150 ml (1/4 pint) milk, 1 egg, 2 stale rolls, 50 g (2 oz) lardon, chopped
parsley, 20 g (3/4 oz) flour, pepper, Worcester sauce.

Dice 2 onions, root vegetables. Sauté in hot oil, add water,
beef bones, salt and cook about 45 minutes. Beat egg with
milk and pinch of salt. Pour mixture over diced rolls. Sauté
finely chopped onion and lardon and add to roll mixture.
Add chopped parsley, mix well and leave to rest for
30 minutes. Work in flour, form small dumplings and cook in
boiling salted water. Strain bouillon, add pepper and
Worcester sauce to taste. Add lardon dumplings before
serving.

Leek Soup

150 g (5 oz) leeks, 1 l (2 pints) stock, 40 g (1 1/2 oz) butter,
60 g (2 1/4 oz) flour, 1/8 l (1/4 pint) milk, 1 egg yolk, nutmeg, chopped
parsley.

Sauté cleaned and sliced leeks in butter, sprinkle with flour,
lightly brown and cover with stock. Mix well and cook for
20 minutes. When soup is ready add milk with blended egg
yolk. Add nutmeg to taste, sprinkle with parsley.

Czech Onion Soup I

2–3 onions, 1 leek, 2 slices of bread, 50 g (2 oz) butter, 400 g (14 oz) beef,
salt, pepper, 2 l (4 pints) water.

Dice bread and sauté in hot butter. Dice beef and cook in
salted peppered water until tender. Meanwhile cut onion and
leek in thin slices. Add onion and leek to soup 15 minutes
before soup is done. When soup is finished fold in egg and
add bread croutons.

Czech Onion Soup II

3–4 onions, 3 medium potatoes, 50 g (2 oz) butter, 50 g (2 oz) flour, 100 g (4oz) Polish sausage, 1 1/2 l (3 pints) water, salt and pepper.

Brown flour lightly in butter. Cover with water and mix well. Add diced potatoes, salt, pepper and cook until tender. Shortly before soup is finished add sliced onions and sausage.

Cauliflower Soup

1 medium cauliflower, 1 1/4 l (2 1/2 pints) water, 40 g (1 1/2 oz) butter, 60 g (2 1/4oz) flour, 1 egg yolk, 1/8 l (1/4 pint) heavy cream, salt, pepper, nutmeg.

Divide washed cauliflower into rosettes and cook in salted water until tender. Remove from water. Lightly brown flour in butter. Add cauliflower water, mix well, and cook 20 minutes. Add cauliflower to soup. Before serving blend in heavy cream and egg yolk. Add pepper and nutmeg to taste.

Mock Turtle Soup

2 Tbsp. semolina, 60 g (2 1/4 oz) butter, 3 carrots, 1 egg, 3/4 l (1 1/2 pints) stock, chopped parsley.

Brown semolina in butter. Add grated carrots and sauté for 5 minutes. Add stock and simmer. When soup is finished fold in egg and sprinkle with chopped parsley.

Sauces

Cream of Dill Sauce

30 g (1 1/4 oz) butter, 1 small bunch of dill weed, 1/4 l (1/2 pint), sweet light cream, 1/4 l (1/2 pint) milk, 60 g (2 1/4 oz) flour, stock, vinegar, salt, sugar.

Shortly boil finely chopped dill weed with 2 Tbsp. of vinegar and 1 Tbsp. of water. Mix light cream with milk. Blend flour in part of milk mixture. Boil rest of milk mixture and gradually add flour, stir constantly for 20 minutes. Add chopped dill weed with butter. If gravy is too thick dilute with stock. Add sugar and salt to taste. Serve over hard boiled eggs or boiled beef with bread dumplings or potatoes.

Horseradish Sauce

60 g (2 1/4 oz) flour, 40 g (1 1/2 oz) butter, 2 l (1/3 pint) milk, 2 l (1/3 pint) sweet light cream, salt, sugar, 30 g (1 1/4 oz) grated horseradish.

Melt butter, add flour and brown lightly. Blend in milk. Stir well and cook 10 minutes. Add light cream and cook another 10 minutes. Add sugar and salt to taste. Fold in grated horseradish. Serve over boiled beef.

Pickled Gherkin Sauce

60 g (2 1/4 oz) butter, 50 g (2 oz) flour, 1/2 l (1 pint) meat stock (beef or chicken), 1 small onion, 150 g (6 oz) pickled gherkins, 0.2 l (1/3 pint) sweet light cream, salt, pepper, sugar, vinegar.

Sauté finely chopped onion in 45 g (1 1/2 oz) butter, sprinkle with flour, brown lightly. Add stock and blend well. Stir often and simmer 20 minutes. Sauté 15 g (3/4 oz) finely chopped gherkins in butter, add to strained sauce. Add salt, pepper, sugar and vinegar to taste.

Garlic Sauce

50 g (2 oz) lard, 60 g (2 1/4 oz) flour, 1 onion, 5 cloves of garlic, stock, salt, pepper.

Sauté finely chopped onion and 2 garlic cloves in lard till golden brown. Sprinkle with flour, brown lightly. Add stock, blend well, and simmer for 20 minute, stirring often. Add pepper. Mash 3 garlic cloves with salt, add to gravy and cook 5 –10 minutes.

Tomato Sauce with Sweet Cream

500 g (16 oz) tomatoes, or 150 g (5 oz) tomato sauce, 50 g (2 oz) flour, 50 g (2 oz) butter, 1 onion, 1/2 tsp. thyme, 1 bay leaf, salt, sugar, vinegar, 1/2 l (1pint) stock, 0.2 l (1/3 pint) sweet cream.

Sauté finely chopped onion in butter. Add thyme, sprinkle with flour and brown lightly. Add sliced tomatoes or tomato sauce and bay leaf. Sauté 5–10 minutes. Add stock-blend well and simmer for 20 minutes. Add cream last. Strain sauce, add salt, sugar and vinegar to taste.

Mushroom Sauce with Sweet Cream

250 g (8 oz) fresh mushrooms, 60 g (2 1/4 oz) flour, 50 g (2 oz) lard, 1 l (1 pint) meat stock, 0.2 l (1/3 pint) sweet cream, 1 onion, salt, pepper, caraway seeds.

Sauté finely chopped onion and thinly sliced mushrooms in lard. Add pepper and caraway seeds. Add stock and simmer. Blend flour with cream, add to sauce, cook 5–10 minutes, and add salt to taste.

Onion Sauce

50 g (2 oz) lard, 60 g (2 1/4 oz) flour, 150 g (5 oz) 1 onion, sugar, vinegar, salt, pepper, 1/2 l (1 pint) meat stock.

Fry finely chopped onions in lard till golden. Sprinkle with flour, brown lightly. Add stock, blend well and simmer. Add salt, pepper, sugar and vinegar to taste.

Cold
Dishes

Sausage in Vinegar Marinade

400 g (14 oz) rope salami (Kielbasa), 2 large onions, 2 small salad cucumbers. Marinade: 2 parts vinegar, 7 parts water, salt, a few peppercorns and allspice, bay leaf, 2 Tbsp. oil, ground pepper.

Bring salted water with spices to a boil, add vinegar and oil. Cool. Skin rope salami and cut in chunks. Peel onion and slice cucumbers thinly. Layer salami, onions and cucumbers in large glass bowl. Cover with marinade. Keep refrigerated for about 3 days. Serve with bread.

Potato Salad

1 kg (2 lbs) potatoes, 200 g (7 oz) ham, 1 onion, 3 sweet / sour gherkins, 4 hard-boiled eggs, 100 g (4 oz) frozen peas, salt, pepper, Worcester sauce, finely chopped parsley, 3 Tbsp. pickle juice, 250 g (8 oz) mayonnaise.

Cook potatoes in skin peel when cooled. Dice potatoes, ham, gherkins and hard-boiled eggs. Finely chop onions, add cooked peas and parsley. Add salt, pepper, pickle juice and a couple of drops of Worcester sauce. Add mayonnaise and stir lightly.

Potato Salad with Marinated Fish

1 kg (2 lb.) potatoes, 2 sweet-sour gherkins, 1 onion, salt, vinegar, mustard, 1 cup sour cream, 2 fillets of marinated fish (herring).

Boil potatoes, peel and dice. Slice fish in narrow strips and dice gherkins. Mix with potatoes, add salt to taste. Blend mustard and finely chopped onion in sour cream. Mix this dressing with potato mixture and fish. Chill for 6 hours.

Fish Fillet Salad

400 g (14 oz) fish fillet, salt, lemon juice, 30 g (1 1/4 oz) butter, 100 g (4 oz) celeriac, 1 onion, 1 hard boiled egg, 300 g (11 oz) mayonnaise, pinch of sugar, Worcester sauce, parsley.

Sauté fish fillet in butter with salt and lemon juice till tender. Cool. Break fish in pieces, add grated celeriac, chopped onion and sliced egg. Mix all ingredients in mayonnaise. Add salt, sugar, Worcester sauce and lemon juice to taste. Chill for 4 hours before serving. Decorate with parsley.

Carp Salad

600 g (20 oz) carp, 4 Tbsp. oil, vinegar, salt, 1 large onion, ground pepper, couple of peppercorns, bay leaf.

Put peppercorns, vinegar and bay leaf in salted water. Bring to boil. Lower heat and add carp. Cook till tender. Bone fish and slice in strips. Add onion cut into thin rings. Add salt, pepper, oil and vinegar to taste. Mix lightly. Chill and serve.

Mushroom Salad

400 g (14 oz) potatoes, 300 g (11 oz) fresh mushrooms, 1 bunch of spring onion, salt, 2 Tbsp. oil, pepper, 5 Tbsp. stock, 20 g (3/4 oz) bacon, 1 clove garlic, 4 Tbsp. vinegar, 1 Tbsp. mustard, parsley.

Cook potatoes in salted water till tender. Meanwhile clean mushrooms and cut in small pieces. Sliceonion including green tops.
Sauté mushrooms in 1 Tbsp. of oil. Add stock and simmer for 5 minutes. Dice bacon and fry till golden. Peel potatoes, slice thinly. While potatoes are still warm add mushrooms, fried bacon with fat. Make marinade from oil, vinegar, crushed garlic and mustard. Add to potato mixture together with sliced onion. Stir salad lightly and chill. Sprinkle with parsley before serving.

Egg Salad with Vegetables

8 hard boiled eggs, 150 g (5 oz) tomatoes, 150 g (5 oz) cucumbers, 1 bell pepper, 1 small onion, 100 g (4 oz) mayonnaise, 100 g (4 oz) plain yogurt, 1Tsp mustard, sugar, pepper, vinegar, salt.

Dice eggs, tomatoes and cucumbers. Slice bell pepper in strips and onions in thin rings. Blend mayonnaise with yogurt. Add mustard, salt, pepper, pinch of sugar and couple drops of vinegar to taste. Mix dressing lightly with salad, chill and serve.

Beef and Horseradish Salad

300 g (11 oz) cooked beef, 2 bell peppers, 2 Tbsp. ketchup, 5 Tbsp. oil, pinch of sugar, pepper, vinegar, salt, grated horseradish.

Cut cooked beef and bell peppers in small strips. Mix ketchup with oil. Add sugar, pepper, vinegar and salt to taste. Add beef and bell peppers. Stir well and leave to rest. Before serving sprinkle with grated horseradish.

Cauliflower Salad

1 medium cauliflower, 2 hard boiled eggs, finely chopped parsley, pinch of sugar, salt, 3 Tbsp. oil, 1 onion, Worcester sauce, 1 Tsp. mustard, vinegar.

Place cauliflower in a pan with salted water and cook until tender. Cool and chop finely. Stir in finely chopped onion. Make marinade using oil, a little water, mustard, vinegar, Worcester sauce, salt and sugar. Mix with cauliflower and onion. Sprinkle finished salad with chopped parsley and finely chopped hard-boiled eggs.

Cauliflower Salad with Tomatoes

1 small cauliflower, salt, 4 medium size firm tomatoes, 1/8-cup (4 oz) heavy whipping cream, 1 Tbsp. grated horseradish, pepper, 1 tsp. sugar, lemon juice.

Divide cauliflower into rosettes and cook in salted water until almost tender (8–10 minutes). Cool. Put tomatoes into boiling water for couple of seconds. Take out, peel and slice. Cover serving plate with cauliflower rosettes and tomato slices. Semi-whip heavy cream and add horseradish, pepper, sugar and lemon juice to taste. Pour cream mixture over cauliflower and tomatoes.

Cheese Spread

100 g (4 oz) grated cheese, 100 g (4 oz) mayonnaise, 4 cloves of garlic, salt.

Mix grated cheese with mayonnaise. Add crushed garlic to taste.

Liptauer Spread

250 g (8 oz) cream cheese, 50 g (2 oz) butter, 1/2 onion, 3 Tbsp. milk, 1 tsp. sweet paprika, salt.

Mix soft butter with cream cheese and milk. Add finely chopped onion, paprika, and salt.

Carrot and Celeriac Spread

200 g (7 oz) carrots, 150 g (5 oz) celeriac, 100 g (4 oz) mayonnaise, lemon juice, sugar, salt and pepper.

Add lemon juice, sugar, salt and pepper to mayonnaise to taste. Finely grate carrots and celeriac. Mix with mayonnaise dressing.

Sardine Spread

150 g (5 oz) soft butter, 1 can of sardines in oil, 5 hard boiled eggs, 1 onion, 3 sweet/sour gherkins, mustard, salt, pepper and lemon juice.

Whip soft butter and sardines until smooth texture. Finely chop hard-boiled eggs, onion, and gherkins. Stir well with sardine butter. Add mustard, salt, pepper and lemon juice to taste.

Crab Spread

250 g (8 oz) crab meat, 150 g (5 oz) mayonnaise, salt, pepper, sugar, lemon juice, slices of lemon for decoration.

Drain crab meat and chop finely. Add salt, pepper, sugar and lemon juice to taste. Leave to rest. Squeeze mixture well. Do not leave any liquid. Mix with mayonnaise and adjust taste.

Tartar Spread

250 g (8 oz) scraped beef (fillet mignon), 1 onion, 2 egg yolks, mustard, ketchup, Worcester sauce, salt, pepper, sweet and hot paprika.

Mix raw scraped meat with mustard, ketchup, Worcester sauce, salt, pepper and paprika. Last add finely chopped onion and egg yolks. Serve tartar spread with slices of dark bread fried in lard. Spread each slice on both sides lightly with crushed garlic. Taste improves if toast is served warm.

Smoked Meat Spread

300 g (11 oz) smoked meat, 100 g (4 oz) mayonnaise, grated horseradish, parsley and salt.

Cook smoked meat until tender. Cool. Cut in small strips, mix with mayonnaise, grated horseradish, chopped parsley. Add salt to taste.

Anchovy Eggs

6 hard boiled eggs, 3 anchovy fillets, 50 g (2 oz) butter, 1 Tbsp. mayonnaise, pepper, 1 Tsp. capers.

Cut peeled hard-boiled eggs lengthwise and take out yolks. Mix chopped anchovy fillets with butter and egg yolks till smooth. Add mayonnaise and pepper. Fill halved eggs with mixture and decorate with capers.

Stuffed Party Loaf

1 loaf of French bread, 250 g (8 oz) soft butter, 5 hard boiled eggs, 1 can sardines in oil, 5 sweet/sour gherkins, 1 onion, 250 g (8 oz) soft salami, 1 red bell pepper, mustard, salt and pepper.

Cut loaf of bread lengthwise and remove soft part. Mix soft butter with sardines till smooth. Finely chop hard-boiled eggs, gherkins, onion, salami, and bell pepper. Blend with sardine butter. Add mustard, salt and pepper to taste. Fill both halves of the bread with this mixture, press together and wrap in aluminum foil. Chill for 24 hours in refrigerator. Cut into thick slices with a sharp knife.

Ham Roll-Ups

300 g (11 oz) ham, 1/4 cup (1/2 pint) heavy whipping cream, 5 Tbsp. grated horseradish, salt and pepper.

Prepare whipping cream, add grated horseradish, salt and pepper. Spread thin slices of ham with horseradish mixture and roll up.

Open Face Party Sandwiches (Chlebicky)

Spread small slices of white party bread with butter or spread and decorate in different fashions.

Different combinations:
1. Mayonnaise, ham, grated horseradish, marinated red pepper, parsley.
2. Butter, ham, hard cheese, marinated red pepper, sweet and sour gherkins.
3. Butter, Italian or Genoa salami, hard-boiled egg, sweet and sour gherkins.
4. Potato salad, ham, hard-boiled eggs, and sweet and sour gherkins.
5. Butter, smoked tongue, hard-boiled eggs, sweet and sour gherkins, hard cheese, parsley.
6. Butter, roast beef, horseradish, whipped cream.
7. Sardine spread, salami, hard-boiled egg, sweet and sour gherkins.
8. Soft herb cheese spread, radishes.
9. Butter, sardine fillets, onion rings.
10. Butter, cod liver, onion rings.

← Roast goose

↑ Beef soup with liver dumplings
↓ Garlic soup

↑ Mushroom gravy with heavy cream
↓ Tomato gravy with heavy cream

Tripe soup

Tripe soup

↑ Sausage in vinegar marinade
↓ Assorted salads

Anchovy eggs

Ham rollups

← Open face party sandwiches (Chlebíčky)

↑ Roast tenderloin (Svíčková)
↓ Roast Beef (Debrecin style)

← Pork on a needle

↑ Beef goulash
↓ Beef rollups

↑ Stuffed pork chops
↓ Stuffed meatloaf

← Czech platter

↑ Carp Southern czech style
↓ Potato pancakes

Breaded champignons

Bread and potato dumplings

← Roast goose

↑ Poppyseed cake
↓ Raised dumplings with blueberries

↑ Bohemian biscuits
↓ Large Domazlice Tart

← Christmas cookies

↑ Brandy cakes
↓ Chocolate cake

Meat
Dishes

Marinated Beef, Znojmo Style

800 g (28 oz) rolled rib roast, 1 large onion, 2 bay leaves, 2 Tbsp. oil, peppercorns, 200 g (7 oz) root vegetables, 2 slices of lemon, 1/4 cup (1/2 pint) vinegar, salt, 20 g (3/4 oz) butter, 2 Tbsp. white wine, flour, 2 sweet and sour gherkins, 1 Tsp. mustard, 1 egg yolk, pepper.

Slice onion and root vegetables. Add 1 pint of water, vinegar, bay leaves, 1 Tsp. oil, peppercorns, vegetables, onion and lemon slices. Cook for 10 minutes. Leave to cool and add roasting beef. Marinate in refrigerator for 2 days. After 2 days take meat out, dry and salt. Add butter to the rest of the oil and fry meat on all sides. Add 1/4 cup (1/2 pint) of strained marinade and wine, also add 2 handfuls of marinated vegetables and simmer until tender. Take out the meat, add flour to the sauce to thicken and simmer shortly. Rub sauce through sieve. Slice gherkins in small strips and add to the sauce together with mustard. Mix egg yolk in small amount of sauce till smooth and add to sauce.

Roast Beef "Znojmo Style"

750 g (1 1/2 lb) rolled rib roast, 30 g (1 1/4 oz) bacon, salt, pepper, 80 g (3 1/4 oz) lard, 3 onions, 1 beef bouillon cube, 30 g (1 1/4 oz) flour, 200 g (7 oz) sweet and sour gherkins, 20 g (3/4 oz) butter.

Lard meat with small pieces of bacon, rub with salt and pepper. Brown finely chopped onion in lard, add meat and brown on all sides. Add part of beef bouillon and simmer slowly until tender. Remove meat from pan, cook gravy and sprinkle with flour. Add rest of the beef bouillon, mix well and simmer. Rub sauce through a sieve. Simmer thinly sliced gherkins in butter, arrange on top of the meat and cover with sauce. Serve with bread dumplings.

Roast Beef with Vegetables

750 g (1 1/2 lb) rump roast, 50 g (2 oz) bacon, 80 g (3 1/4 oz) lard,
150 g (5 oz) root vegetables, salt, pepper, 1 onion, 30 g (1 1/4 oz) flour,
1/2 cube of beef bouillon.

Lard meat with small pieces of bacon, rub with salt and
pepper. Brown on all sides in lard. Remove browned meat
and add chopped root vegetables and onion to lard and
brown lightly. Put meat back on browned vegetables, add
1 cup water, cover and roast until tender. Turn meat during
roasting and add bouillon as needed. Remove tender meat,
dust dripping with flour, add more bouillon, stir well and
simmer. Rub gravy through strainer, pour over sliced meat.
Serve with potatoes or rice.

Roast Tenderloin (Svickova)

750 g (1 1/2 lb) tenderloin of beef, 100 g (4 oz) bacon, 300 g (11 oz) root
vegetables (carrot, celeriac, parsnip), grated lemon peel, 2 onions, 3 bay
leaves, 2 tsp. thyme, peppercorn, 1 pint whipping cream, 1 Tbsp. flour,
vinegar or lemon juice, 100 g (4 oz) butter, salt and pepper.

After removing meat membranes, lard with 1/2-inch thick
strips of bacon. Slice root vegetables and onion thinly. Melt
butter and cool. Cover bottom of roasting pan with bacon
strips and half of the sliced vegetables. Put meat on top of
vegetables and season with thyme, pepper, lemon peel and
bay leaves. Cover with rest of the sliced vegetables and
melted butter. Chill overnight. Add salt just before roasting.
Roast in oven until tender, basting frequently with it's own
juices, adding more water as needed. Remove meat from pan,
press gravy and vegetables through a strainer, add whipping
cream with flour to strained gravy and simmer. Add vinegar
or lemon juice to taste. Serve with bread dumplings and
cranberry relish.

Roast Beef "Debrecin Style"

1 kg (2 lb) rump roast, 2 frankfurters, 30 g (1 1/4 oz) bacon, salt, pepper, 4 onions, 100 g (4 oz) lard, 1/4 l (1/2 pint) bouillon, 20 g (3/4 oz) flour, 20 g (3/4 oz) butter, 1 tsp. sweet paprika.

Lard meat with bacon and frankfurters cut into strips lengthwise. Brown chopped onions lightly in lard. Add meat, salt and pepper. Brown well on all sides. Add part of bouillon, cover and roast until tender, basting often. Remove meat from pan, dust dripping with flour, add rest of bouillon and simmer. Strain gravy and add sweet paprika mixed with melted butter. Serve with potatoes or bread dumplings.

Stuffed Roast Beef

Meat
Dishes

1 kg (2 lb) rump roast, salt, pepper, 30 g (1 1/4 oz) bacon, 150 g (5 oz) smoked meat, 100 g (4 oz) sweet sour gherkins, 2 hard-boiled eggs, 30 g (3 1/4 oz) lard, 4 onions, 1/4 l (1/2 pint) bouillon, 30 g (1 1/4 oz) flour, mustard.

Pound meat lightly and add salt and pepper. Lard with strips of bacon, smoked meat and gherkins. Slice roast lengthwise, making a pocket. Spread meat pocket with mustard and fill with peeled hard-boiled eggs, fasten with skewers or toothpicks. Brown well in lard on all sides, add chopped onion, bouillon and roast, basting often, until tender. Remove meat from pan, dust dripping with flour and add rest of bouillon, simmer. Strain gravy and add rest of gherkins and smoked meat. Serve with potatoes.

Large Rolled Beef – I

1 kg (2 lb) round steak, salt, pepper, mustard, 1 clove of garlic,
pinch of marjoram, 100 g (4 oz) ham salami, 50 g (2 oz) bacon,
3 eggs, 2 sweet sour gherkins, 150 g (5 oz) root vegetables, 2 onions,
120 g (4 oz) lard, 2 tomatoes, 30 g (1 1/4 oz) flour, 1/4 l (1/2 pint) bouillon.

Pound meat well, sprinkle with salt and pepper. Spread with
mustard and season with pressed garlic and marjoram.
Cover with thinly sliced ham salami and bacon. Make omelet
with 3 eggs, spread over bacon and top with sliced gherkins.
Roll meat, fasten with skewers or toothpicks. Brown chopped
root vegetables and onion in lard, add sliced tomatoes. Put
rolled beef on top of browned vegetables, add bouillon and
roast, basting often. Remove tender meat from pan, dust
gravy with flour, add rest of bouillon and simmer. Strain
gravy. Serve with potatoes or rice.

Large Rolled Beef – II.

1 kg (2 lb) round steak, 80 g (3 oz) butter, 1 onion, 30 g (1 1/4 oz) flour,
1/4 l (1/2 pint) bouillon.
Stuffing: 500 g (1 lb) minced beef and pork, 2 anchovy fillets, 1 egg, salt,
pepper, 1 small onion, 3 hard boiled eggs.

Pound meat well, sprinkle with salt and pepper. Add 1 egg,
salt, pepper, chopped onion, and chopped anchovy fillets to
minced meat, mix well. Spread meat mixture over pounded
beef, top with hard-boiled eggs. Roll meat, fasten with
skewers or toothpicks. Brown chopped onion in butter, add
rolled beef and brown well on all sides. Add bouillon and
roast till tender. Remove meat, dust gravy with flour and
simmer.

Rolled Beef Steaks "Budweiser Style"

4 slices 3/4 inch thick round steak, 250 g (8 oz) rice, 2 eggs,
30 g (1 1/4 oz) dried mushrooms, 1 large onion, 1 cup whipping
cream, 80 g (3 oz) butter, 20 g (3/4 oz) flour, 100 g (4 oz) root vegetables,
salt, pepper, bay leaf and lemon juice.

Pound meat sprinkle with salt and pepper. Brown finely chopped sautéed mushrooms, cooked rice and eggs in butter. Cover each steak with this mixture. Roll meat and fasten with toothpicks. Sauté chopped onion and root vegetables in butter. Add meat to pan and brown quickly on all sides. Add 1 cup of water, cover and simmer until tender. Blend in whipping cream and lemon juice to taste. Strain sauce.

Beef Roll-Ups I

4 slices 3/4 inch thick top round steaks, salt, pepper, mustard, 30 g (1 1/4 oz) bacon, 2 frankfurters, 2 eggs, 2 sweet sour gherkins, 3 onions, 80 g (3 oz) lard, bouillon, flour.

Pound steaks, sprinkle with salt, pepper and spread with mustard. Cover with sliced bacon, frankfurters and gherkins. Put 1/2 of hard-boiled egg on each steak. Roll meat and fasten with skewers. Dust roll-ups with flour and brown well in lard on all sides. Remove meat, brown finely chopped onion and place roll-ups back in pan. Add bouillon and simmer until tender. Remove roll-ups again, strain gravy and add mustard to taste. Serve with potatoes or bread dumplings.

Beef Roll-Ups II

4 slices 3/4 inch thick round steak, 150 g (5 oz) minced pork, 2 anchovy fillets, 50 g (2 oz) butter, 1 egg, salt and pepper, 100 g (4 oz) bacon, 400 g (14 oz) root vegetables, bay leaf, grated lemon peel, 100 g (4 oz) sour cream, flour.

Mix soft butter with finely chopped anchovy fillets until smooth. Add egg, minced pork and salt and pepper to taste. Pound steaks, sprinkle with salt and pepper. Spread with meat mixture, roll up and fasten with skewers. Line pan with bacon, add rolled meat, finely chopped root vegetables, bay leaf and grated lemon peel. Simmer slowly, adding stock as needed. Remove roll-ups, press gravy with vegetables through sieve, add sour cream with flour. Simmer gravy and add salt to taste. Serve with bread dumplings.

Roast Beef Cooked in Beer

800 g (28 oz) rump roast, salt, pepper, 3/8 l (12 fluid ozs) dark beer, 1 onion, 3 Tbsp. oil, pinch of thyme, 2 Tbsp. tomato sauce, 3 Tbsp. breadcrumbs.

Sprinkle roast with salt and pepper. Put in bowl and cover with beer. Marinate in refrigerator till next day. Turn meat several times. Brown onions lightly in oil, add wiped meat and brown on all sides. Add beer marinade, salt, pepper, thyme, and tomato sauce. Cover and roast. Remove tender meat, thicken gravy with breadcrumbs and simmer. Serve with potatoes.

Roast Beef in "Robe"

4 slices cooked beef, 8 slices gouda cheese, mustard, flour, 2 eggs, breadcrumbs and oil.

Spread sliced cheese with mustard. Place one slice of beef between two slices of cheese, fasten with skewers. Roll in flour, beaten salted eggs and breadcrumbs. Brown on both sides in hot oil. Serve with mashed potatoes and green salad.

Beef Goulash

750 g (1 1/2 lb) beef chuck, 400 g (14 oz) onion, 6 Tbsp. oil, salt, pepper, sweet paprika, marjoram, caraway seeds, 5 cloves of garlic, 1 small can of tomato paste, 1/2 l (1 pint) hot water, 1 slice dark bread, onion rings for decoration.

Cut meat in small cubes, chop onion and slice garlic. Brown meat in hot oil and add onion and garlic. Continue to brown. Add salt and pepper, paprika, tomato paste, caraway seeds, and marjoram. Simmer, adding hot water as needed. Cut bread in small cubes, add to goulash and simmer until bread dissolves. Serve with bread dumplings, decorate with onion rings.

Pork Roast

1 kg (2 lb) pork loin, salt, caraway seeds, 4 cloves of garlic,
50 g (2 oz) lard, 1 small onion, 15 g (1 Tbsp.) flour, 1/4 l (1/2 pint) bouillon.

Rub meat with crushed garlic and sprinkle with caraway seeds. Add cup of water and halved onion, to be discarded later. Baste meat often, adding bouillon as needed. Turn meat during roasting. If meat is too lean, add lard to pan juices. Remove meat from pan, dust gravy with flour, add rest of bouillon and simmer. Serve with bread dumplings and sauerkraut.

Sauerkraut

400 g (14 oz) sauerkraut, 1 tsp. caraway seeds, 1 onion,
40 g (1 1/2 oz) lard, 1 raw potato, 1 tsp. flour, sugar and salt.

Put sauerkraut in wide pot, add caraway seeds, cup of hot water and simmer. Brown finely chopped onion in lard. Peel potato and grate finely, add to onion, dust with flour. Fold onion mixture into sauerkraut and simmer until tender. Add salt and sugar to taste.

Czech Platter

This meal is ideal for a larger number of people. They can try several classic Czech dishes at one time.
Mount sauerkraut and red cabbage in the center of a large serving platter, adding slices of smoked meat, meat loaf and roast pork. Serve with bread and potato dumplings.
Serve sauce separately.

Pork Kabobs

500 g (1 lb) pork tenderloin, 50 g (2 oz) bacon, 2 onions

Marinade: 8 Tbsp. oil, 1 tsp. salt, 1/2 tsp. pepper, 2 crushed cloves of garlic.

Cut meat in cubes, bacon in thin slices. Peel onion, cut in quarters and take apart. Loosely thread pork chunks on skewers, alternately with bacon and onion. Dip kabobs in marinade, roast for 20 minutes or grill, turning often.

Leg of Pork "Hunter's Style"

1 kg (2 lb) leg of pork, salt, 1/2 l (1 pint) water, vinegar, 3 whole peppercorns, 2 whole allspice, 1 bay leaf, 200 g (7 oz) root vegetables, 2 onions, 120 g (4 oz) butter, 40 g (1 1/2 oz) flour, 1/8 l (4 oz) white wine, 1 lemon, 3 Tbsp. red currant jam.

Remove membranes from meat and rub with salt.
To prepare marinade: Boil water with vinegar, salt, add seasoning and sliced root vegetables and onions. Simmer briefly. Put meat in large bowl and cover with cooled marinade, cover and chill in refrigerator for 1–2 days. Turn meat several times. Take vegetables out of marinade and fry till light brown in butter, add meat and brown on all sides. Roast slowly until tender, basting with marinade. Remove meat, dust gravy with flour, add rest of marinade and wine, lemon juice to taste. Last add jam, simmer shortly and rub through sieve. Serve with bread dumplings.

Leg of Pork in Cream Sauce

500 g (1 lb.) leg of pork, salt, 30 g (1 1/4 oz) bacon, 100 g (4 oz) smoked meat, 100 g (4 oz) sweet-sour gherkins, 100 g (4 oz) root vegetables, 1 onion, 60 g (2 1/4 oz) lard, 3 whole peppercorns, 2 whole allspice, 1 bay leaf, 30 g (1 1/4 oz) flour, 1/4 l (1/2 pint) whipping cream, 1 lemon, sugar.

Lard meat with sliced bacon, smoked meat and gherkins. Rub with salt. Brown finely chopped root vegetables and

onion in lard, add meat and brown on all sides. Add seasoning, water and simmer until tender. Remove meat, dust gravy with flour, add more water as needed and simmer. Last add whipping cream and rub sauce through a sieve.
Serve with bread dumplings.

Rolled Pork with Herb Stuffing

700 g (1 1/2 lb) pork shoulder, 1 bunch of herbs (parsley, chives, marjoram), salt, 4 cloves of garlic, 1 egg, pepper, 1 tbsp. bread crumbs, 6 Tbsp. whipping cream, sweet paprika, 1 onion, 3 slices lemon, 20 g (3/4 oz) butter, 1/2 l (1 pint) bouillon, 1 slice toast.

Have meat cut in a slice about 3/4 inch thick. Finely chop all herbs and 2 cloves of garlic, mix with egg, breadcrumbs and 1 Tbsp. of whipping cream, add salt, pepper and paprika to taste. Cover meat with herb mixture, roll up and tie tightly. Add more salt and pepper as needed. Put meat in roasting pan, add 2 cloves of garlic, coarsely chopped onion and lemon slices. While roasting, baste often with bouillon and butter. Remove meat from pan. Cut crust off toast, crumble and add to strained gravy. Stir until bread dissolves. Add rest of the whipping cream and salt, pepper and paprika to taste.
Serve with potatoes.

Rolled Pork with Mushrooms

700 g (1 1/2 lb.) pork shoulder, mustard, salt, 80 g (3 oz) ham, 2 onions, 3 anchovy fillets, 1 bunch of parsley, thyme, pepper, 1 egg, 20 g (3/4 oz) bacon, 1 Tbsp. oil, 1/2 l (1 pint) red wine, 200 g (7 oz) mushrooms, potato flour.

Have meat cut in a slice about 3/4 inch thick, spread with mustard. Finely chop ham, onions, anchovy fillets and parsley. Mix ham with anchovies, egg and half the onion and parsley. Add thyme, salt and pepper to taste. Spread mixture over meat slice, roll up and tie tightly. Rub with salt and pepper. Fry finely chopped bacon in hot oil, add rolled meat and brown on all sides. Add wine, cover and simmer slowly.

Clean and slice mushrooms, add to meat after 45 minutes together with a pinch of thyme. Simmer until meat is tender. Remove meat from pan, thicken gravy with potato flour, simmer and add rest of the parsley.
Serve with bread dumplings.

Roast Pork with Horseradish

1 kg (2 lb) pork loin, salt, pepper, sweet paprika, caraway seeds, 2 tsp. potato flour, 2 Tbsp. sour cream, 2 Tbsp. grated horseradish.

Rub meat with salt, pepper, paprika and sprinkle with caraway seeds. Add cup of hot water and roast. Baste often, adding water as it evaporates. Remove tender meat, add water to gravy to make 1/2 l (1 pint) and bring to boil. Lower heat, add sour cream mixed with potato flour, simmer. At the end of cooking add grated horseradish.
Serve with bread dumplings.

Roast Pork with Prunes

750 g (1 1/2 lb) pork shoulder with skin, 5 pitted prunes, salt, pepper, 1 onion, 2 cloves, 2 Tbsp. oil, 1/8 l (4 fluid oz) whipping cream.

Cut prunes in quarters and soak in 1/8 l (4 oz) of water overnight. Slash pork skin, rub meat with salt and pepper. Put in hot oil, skin down, add 1/4 l (1/2 pint) of water and roast for 20 minutes. Turn meat and add peeled onion pierced with cloves. Baste often and roast until tender. Remove meat from pan, add prunes and whipping cream to the gravy. Cook down to 1/4 l (1/2 pint) of gravy.
Serve with noodles.

Stuffed Pork Chops

4 thick pork chops, 100 g (4 oz) gouda cheese, 1 tsp. estaragon, 2 tsp. mustard, salt, pepper, oil, herb butter.

Cut cheese in small cubes. Pound meat and cut side pocket. Spread with mustard and fill with cheese cubes and estragon, fasten pocket with skewers. Rub with salt and pepper. Brown chops in hot oil, turning several times.
Serve decorated with herb butter.

Pork Chops with Mustard

4 pork chops, salt, 80 g (3 oz) lard, 2 onions, 1 Tbsp. mustard, 1/2 lemon, 30 g (1 1/4 oz) flour.

Pound chops, slash edges, sprinkle with salt and fry in lard on both sides. Remove from pan. Add coarsely chopped onion, mustard and grated lemon peel. Put chops back in pan, add a little water and simmer. Dust tender chops with flour, add more water and remove from pan. Stir gravy well, simmer briefly and rub through a sieve.
Serve with potatoes.

Pork Chops with Mushrooms

4 pork chops, salt, pepper, caraway seeds, 60 g (2 1/4 oz) lard, 1 onion, 30 g (1 1/4 oz) flour, 1/4 l (1/2 pint) bouillon, 150 g (6 oz) fresh mushrooms, 100 g (4 oz) butter.

Pound chops, slash edges. Sprinkle with salt and pepper, fry in lard on both sides. Add finely chopped onion, some of the bouillon and simmer until tender. Remove meat, dust gravy with flour, add rest of the bouillon and simmer. Clean and slice mushrooms, sauté in butter. Add salt and caraway seeds, add to gravy and simmer shortly.
Serve with rice or bread dumplings.

Pork Chops with Paprikakraut

4 pork chops, salt, pepper, caraway seeds, oil, 1 large red bell pepper,
1 can of sauerkraut, 1/8 l (4 oz) bouillon, 4 slices edam cheese.

Pound chops and fry in hot oil on both sides (about
6 minutes). Sprinkle with salt, pepper and caraway seeds.
Remove chops, cover and keep warm. Slice bell pepper and
sauté shortly in oil, add sauerkraut and bouillon, simmer for
10 minutes. Arrange chops on top of sauerkraut, top each
chop with a slice of cheese, cover and allow cheese to melt.

Pork Medallions with Herbed Potatoes

800 g (28 oz) potatoes, 2 cloves of garlic, 1 Tbsp. butter, salt, pepper, 1 tsp.
marjoram, 2/10 l (4 Tbsp.) whipping cream, 1/8 l (4 oz) milk, 8 thin slices of
bacon, 8 pork medallions, 1/8 l (4 oz) dry red wine, 1/8 l (4 oz) bouillon,
2–3 Tbsp. sour cream, 1 bunch of parsley.

Cut peeled potatoes in thick slices, finely chop garlic, melt
butter in wide pot. Sauté potatoes and garlic in butter, add
salt, pepper and marjoram to taste. Add whipping cream and
milk, bring to boil, cover and simmer for 10–15 minutes until
tender. Meanwhile fry bacon crisp. Keep warm. Fry pork
medallions in bacon fat, remove from pan and keep warm.
Add red wine, bouillon, sour cream to bacon fat, bring to
boil, stirring constantly.
Arrange medallions on plates. Cover with gravy. Decorate
with crisp bacon and serve with herbed potatoes, sprinkle
with finely chopped parsley.

Pork Roll-Ups with Mushrooms

4 pork slices, salt, 150 g (6 oz) mushrooms, 30 g (1 1/4 oz) butter, lemon
juice, pepper, caraway seeds, 1/2 cup white wine, 2 eggs, breadcrumbs,
50 g (2 oz) butter, 30 g (1 1/4 oz) flour, 1/4 l (1/2 pint) bouillon.

Pound meat, sprinkle with salt. Clean and slice mushrooms,
sauté in butter. Add lemon juice, salt, caraway seeds and
wine. Beat eggs, add to mushrooms, sprinkle with

breadcrumbs, stir and leave to set. Spread meat slices with mushroom mixture, roll up and tie. Brown in butter, add bouillon and simmer until tender. Remove roll-ups, dust gravy with flour, add rest of the bouillon and simmer. Serve with rice or potatoes.

Pork Schnitzels "Brno Style"

4 pork cutlets, 20 g (3/4 oz) butter, 80 g (3 oz) ham, 50 g (2 oz) of canned green peas, salt, pepper, 1 egg. Coating mixture: 50 g (2 oz) flour, 2 eggs, 100 g (4 oz) breadcrumbs.

Pound meat lightly, cut side pocket in each cutlet. Mix finely chopped ham, drained peas and egg, sauté in butter until set. Add salt and pepper to taste. Fill meat pockets with this mixture and sprinkle with salt. Fasten with skewers. Dip first in flour, then in beaten salted eggs then in breadcrumbs. Fry in hot butter until golden brown. Serve with potatoes.

Pork Schnitzels with Horseradish

4 thin pork cutlets, salt, pepper, 50 g (2 oz) grated horseradish, 50 g (2 oz) flour, 2 eggs, 100 g (4 oz) breadcrumbs.

Pound meat, sprinkle with salt and pepper. Spread grated horseradish on top of each cutlet-press in with fingers. Dip bottom side of meat in flour, drizzle top with eggs. Dip in breadcrumbs, sprinkle top with breadcrumbs. Press firmly together, rest for about 10 minutes. Fry cutlets, horseradish side down first, then turn and fry other side.
Serve with potatoes.

Cabbage Rolls with Minced Pork

1 cabbage, 2 Tbsp. lard, 150 g (6 oz) finely chopped onion,
500 g (1lb) minced pork, 2 eggs, 2 Tbsp. sweet paprika, marjoram, salt,
pepper, 3/4 cup cooked rice, 1 tsp. finely chopped garlic,
1 kg (2 lb) sauerkraut, 50 g (2 oz) lard, 1 cup of tomato paste (mixed with
1 cup of water) 50 g (2 oz) butter, 50 g (2 oz) flour, 1.2 l (1 pint) sour cream.

Boil head of cabbage in salted water for about 10 minutes.
Remove large outer leaves for stuffing. Brown finely chopped
onion in lard. In large bowl mix minced pork, eggs, paprika,
marjoram, salt, pepper, rice, brown onion and garlic. Place
about 2 Tbsp. of this mixture on each cabbage leaf, roll,
folding lightly. Make roll-ups, using all the stuffing. Cover
bottom of pyrex dish with sauerkraut, top with cabbage roll-
ups on warm platter. Leave sauerkraut in pyrex dish. Melt
butter and dust with flour.

Meat
Dishes

Stuffed Meat Loaf

1 kg (2 lb) minced beef and pork, 2 rolls, 1/8 l (4 oz) milk, 2 eggs,
30 g (1 1/4 oz) bacon, 1 onion, salt, pepper, marjoram, 1 Tbsp. mustard,
2 cloves of garlic, breadcrumbs.

Stuffing: 4 hard-boiled eggs, 2 frankfurters.

Minced meat, rolls soaked in milk, 1 egg, 2 egg yolks (save
1 egg white for meat loaf glaze), chopped bacon, chopped
onion, salt, pepper, marjoram, mustard, crushed garlic and
some breadcrumbs. Mix all ingredients well. Form two loaves
with wet hands . Hollow each loaf lengthwise and fill with
hard-boiled eggs and frankfurters.
Form loaves again. Brush with egg white, put in pan with cup
of hot water and roast, basting often. Add hot water as
needed. Remove meat loaf from pan when done, dust gravy
with flour, add water and simmer.
Serve with potatoes or mashed potatoes.

Boiled Smoked Meat

1 kg (2 lbs) smoked meat, 50 g (2 oz) root vegetables, 1 onion.

Put meat in boiling water, add sliced root vegetables and onion. Cook until tender. Slice meat and serve with sauerkraut and potato dumplings. Sprinkle dumplings with finely chopped browned onion and melted lard.

Noodle Casserole with Smoked Meat

500 g (1 lb) wide noodles, salt, 300 g (12 oz) smoked meat, 1 onion, butter, 3 eggs, 1 cup of milk, pepper.

Meat
Dishes

Break up noodles, boil in salted water with some oil. When done, strain and rinse in cold water. Brown finely chopped onion in butter. Mix cooked chopped smoked meat with browned onion and noodles. Add salt and pepper to taste. Put into a well-greased casserole sprinkled with breadcrumbs. Bake until top turns golden, cover with eggs beaten in salted milk and continue to bake until top is golden brown.

Liver Sausage

250 g (10 oz) meat from pig's head, 1 pig's lungs and heart,
200 g (8 oz) pork liver, 2–3 rolls, 1 cup stock, salt, pepper, marjoram, dash of ground allspice, 1 mashed clove of garlic, dash of ginger, lard.

Simmer meat in salted water until tender. Soak the rolls in stock and squeeze almost dry. Chop cooked meat, rolls and raw liver and mince coarsely. Add marjoram, pepper, allspice, garlic, and ginger. Add salt to taste. Mix well, pour into a greased pan and bake for about 45 minutes until golden. Serve with potatoes and sauerkraut.

Easter Pudding

500 g (1 lb) pork shoulder, 500 g (1 lb) smoked meat, 6 eggs,
500 g (1 lb) stale rolls, 3/4 l (1 1/2 pints) stock, 2 Tbsp. milk,
50 g (2 oz) yeast, 2 cloves of garlic, pepper, nutmeg, marjoram, salt, pinch
of sugar, 1 bunch of parsley, 1 bunch of chives, 1 bunch of young nettles.

Cook meat in salted water, cut in small cubes. Cut rolls also
in small cubes and soak in meat stock. Mix milk, yeast and
sugar, leave to rise. Separate egg yolks from egg whites. Mix
cubed meat, rolls, egg yolks, finely chopped parsley, chives
and nettles. Add yeast mixture. Add salt, pepper, nutmeg,
marjoram and mashed garlic. Also add stiffly beaten egg
whites. Pour mixture into greased pudding form. Leave to
rise for about 30 minutes. Bake until golden.

Fish

Breaded Carp

1 carp (about 1 1/2 kg-3 lbs), salt, lemon juice, 100 g (4 oz) flour, 2 eggs, 100 g (4 oz) breadcrumbs, oil.

Sprinkle dried salted portions of carp with lemon juice. Roll in flour, dip in lightly beaten eggs and roll in breadcrumbs. Fry slowly in large amount of oil. Serve with wedges of lemon and potato salad.

Carp with Cheese Sauce

1 carp (1 1/2 kg-3 lbs) 1 l (2 pints) water, 1/8 l (4 oz) white wine, 4 peppercorns, salt, parsley.

Sauce: 2 Tbsp. flour, 1 onion, 50 g (2 oz) butter, 1/4 l (1/2 pint) heavy cream, 50 g (2 oz) grated cheese, pepper, salt, nutmeg.

Cut carp into serving pieces. Add wine, peppercorns and parsley to salted water, simmer carp in this liquid for about 15 minutes. Remove tender fish with care. Brown flour, finely chopped onion in butter, add fish stock and heavy cream. Blend well and simmer. Add grated cheese, salt, pepper, and nutmeg to taste. Cover fish pieces with cheese sauce, decorate with parsley and serve with potatoes.

Fish

Stuffed Carp

1 carp (2 kg – 4 lbs), 300 g (11 oz) champignons, 1 onion, salt, pepper, 6 Tbsp. Butter, 2 Tbsp. flour, 2 Tbsp. finely chopped parsley, 1/8 l (4 oz) white wine.

Clean carp. Slice champignons and sauté with finely chopped onion in butter for 5 minutes. Add salt to taste. Sprinkle fish inside and out with salt and pepper, fill with champignons, fasten with skewers. Roll carp in flour, put into pan, greased with butter, drizzle with

3 Tbsp. of melted butter. Roast for about 40 minutes, turn once. Sauté finely chopped parsley in butter, add wine, simmer, add salt and pepper to taste. Use this as a basting liquid during baking.
Serve with potatoes. Sprinkle with parsley.

Carp with Champignons

4 pieces of carp, 3 cloves of garlic, salt, 1 cup white wine, peppercorn, nutmeg, parsley.

Gravy: 100 g (4 oz) butter, 1 small onion, 100 g (4 oz) champingons, lemon juice, 20 g (3.4 oz) flour, 200 g (8 oz) tomatoes, 1 egg yolk.

Spread carp with crushed garlic. Place in a pan, add wine, some water, peppercorn, pinch of nutmeg and parsley. Simmer for about 10 minutes. Remove tender fish with care and keep warm. Brown finely chopped onion in butter, add sliced champignons and drizzle with lemon juice. Simmer briefly, dust with flour, add fish stock and simmer. Place tomatoes in boiling water, peel, halve, remove seeds and dice. Add to champignons and simmer briefly. Mix in egg yolk. Serve with potatoes or rice.

Carp South Czech Style

4 pieces of carp, 80 g (3 oz) butter, 1 onion, 1 cup sour cream, 500 g (1 lb) potatoes, salt, sweet paprika, parsley.

Brown finely chopped onion, add peeled, sliced potatoes, salt to taste. Cut pocket in each piece of carp and fill of with shaves butter. Salt. Place fish on top of potatoes, sprinkle with paprika and parsley. Add sour cream and bake for about 20 minutes.

Fish Fillet with Ham and Cheese

500 g (1 lb) fish fillet, salt, lemon juice, 100 g (4 oz) ham, 100 g (4 oz) flour, 2 eggs, 100 g (4 oz) breadcrumbs, 100 g (4 oz) grated cheese, oil.

Cut fish fillet into thin slices, add salt and lemon juice. Place thin slice of ham between 2 fish slices, fasten with toothpicks. Roll in flour, dip in beaten salted eggs and roll in breadcrumbs mixed with grated cheese. Fry in oil until golden brown. Serve with potatoes or mashed potatoes.

Moravian Fish Loaf

1 kg (2 lbs) boneless fish (raw or cooked), 50 g (2 oz) bacon, 1 large onion, Brussels sprouts, 1 roll, 2 Tbsp. milk, 1 large cooked potato, 1 egg, salt, pepper, breadcrumbs.

Brown finely chopped onion with bacon. Add Brussels sprouts, sauté. Allow to cool and mix with fish using blender. Add roll soaked in milk and cooked potatoes. Add salt, pepper, egg and breadcrumbs as needed. Line greased pan with onion rings. Form loaf and wrap in aluminium foil. Bake until onion rings darken, add some water to the pan. Serve with potatoes.

Fish

Fowl and Game

Chicken with Stuffing

1 chicken, salt, pepper

Stuffing: 3 rolls, 1 cup milk, 3 eggs, 50 g (2 oz) butter, nutmeg, parsley, breadcrumbs, salt.

Dice rolls and soak in milk blended with beaten egg yolks. Add melted butter, chopped parsley, nutmeg and salt. Fold in stiff beaten egg whites carefully. Sprinkle chicken with salt and pepper and fill with stuffing. Rub with butter and add any remaining butter to roasting pan. Roast chicken until golden brown. Serve with roast potatoes.

Chicken with Herbs

1 chicken, salt, 20 g (3/4 oz) butter, 4 tomatoes, 2 cloves of garlic, pepper, marjoram, thyme, basil, 1 Tbsp. flour, 1 Tbsp. tomato paste, parsley.

Cut chicken into small pieces, salt and brown in butter on all sides. Put in pan, add peeled diced tomatoes, crushed garlic, pepper, marjoram, thyme and basil. Add water and roast. Remove tender chicken from pan, dust gravy with flour, add more water, tomato paste and finely chopped parsley, simmer briefly.
Serve with potatoes or rice.

Chicken with Mushrooms

1 chicken, 50 g (2 oz) butter, 1 onion, 100 g (6 oz) fresh mushrooms, 1/4 l (1/2 pint) sour cream, 2 Tbsp. flour, salt.

Cut chicken into four pieces, brown in butter, add finely chopped onion and simmer. Then salt meat, add hot water, sliced mushrooms, simmer until tender. Remove chicken from pan. Mix sour cream and flour together, blend into pan juices and bring gravy to a boil.
Serve with rice.

Chicken Paprika

1 chicken, 1 onion, 50 g (2 oz) butter, 40 g (1 1/2 oz) flour,
1/4 l (1/2 pint) whipping cream, sweet paprika, salt.

Cut chicken into small pieces, salt. Brown finely chopped
onion in butter, add chicken pieces and brown on both sides.
Dust with paprika, add water, cover and simmer until tender.
Take out chicken and remove bones. Mix whipping cream
with flour, stir into gravy and simmer for 5 minutes. Add
pieces of chicken.
Serve with bread dumplings.

Chicken Stuffed with Vegetable Paste

1 chicken, salt, pepper, hot paprika, 1 bell pepper, 1 bunch of spring onions,
3 Tbsp. milk, 2 cloves of garlic, oil, sweet paprika, 1 Tbsp. honey.

Sprinkle chicken with salt and pepper, rub with hot paprika.
Finely chop bell pepper and spring onion, mix with soft
butter, add crushed garlic, salt and pepper. Stuff chicken
with vegetable paste and tie. Roast. 15 minutes before it is
done baste chicken with oil, sweet paprika and honey
marinade.

Chicken Meat Casserole (Trochanek)

500 g (16 oz) chicken giblets, root vegetables, salt, 2 eggs, 12 Tbsp. flour.

Cook meat in salted water with root vegetables. Remove
tender meat and chop. Add spices. Work eggs and flour into
a firm dough (not using water if possible), put dough for 1
hour into refrigerator. Grate dough coarsely on to a dry
baking sheet and bake until golden brown. Cool, crumble
with your fingers, add spiced broth and meat. Broth should
be about 1 inch above the dough and meat mixture. Mix well
and bake for about 1 hour, till broth soaks in.

Stuffed Roast Turkey

1 turkey (about 6–7 lbs), salt, 100 g (4 oz) butter, 100 g (4 oz) bacon,
2 Tbsp flour.
Stuffing: 60 g (2 1/4 oz) butter, 4 anchovy fillets, 2 eggs, 1 egg
yolk, 500 g (1 lb) minced pork, 1 turkey liver, pepper, grated lemon
rind, 60 g (2 1/4 oz) breadcrumbs.

Lard turkey with bacon, rub with salt. Blend soft butter with
chopped anchovies, mix with eggs, egg yolk, minced pork,
chopped liver and breadcrumbs. Add pepper and grated
lemon rind to taste. Stuff body and neck cavities, close with
skewers or sew. Rub turkey with butter, place in pan, add
water and roast. Add water as needed, baste frequently.
Remove tender turkey, dust pan juices with flour, boil down,
add hot water and simmer.
Serve with potatoes and fruit relish.

Roast Goose or Duck

1 goose, salt, 1 Tbsp flour, caraway seeds.

Clean and wash goose, sprinkle with salt and caraway seeds
inside and out. Place into a roasting pan breast down, add
1 cup water and roast. During roasting pierce skin several
times, skim off excess fat and add more hot water as needed.
Roast goose for 1 hour for each 2 lbs. of meat, turning once.
Remove tender bird, boil down pan juices, dust with flour,
boil down again. Add hot water, mix well and simmer.
Prepare duck in the same way.
Serve goose with sauerkraut and bread dumplings.
Serve duck with red cabbage and potato dumplings.

White Cabbage

Medium size white cabbage, 40 g (1 1/2 oz) lard, 1 Tbsp. flour, 1 onion,
1 Tbsp. caraway seeds, vinegar, sugar, and salt.

Cut cabbage in quarters, remove heart and outer leaves.
Slice into fine strips, boil in salted water with caraway seeds

until tender. Drain. Brown finely chopped onion in lard, dust with flour and blend into cooked cabbage, simmer shortly. Add vinegar, sugar and salt to taste.

Roast Turkey Legs with Horseradish

2 turkey legs (each about 1 lb.) 2 bunches of soup vegetables, 1 parsnip, 2 onions, 3 Tbsp oil, salt, pepper, 2 bay leaves.

Coating paste: 130 g (5 oz) grated horseradish, 1 lemon, salt, pepper, 2 bunches of parsley, 2 egg yolks, 3 Tbsp sour cream, 4 Tbsp breadcrumbs, Worcester sauce.

Slice soup vegetables and parsnip, cut onion in quarters, sauté in hot oil. Add 2 l (4 pints) water, salt, pepper and bay leaves, cover and simmer for 15 minutes. Place turkey legs in vegetable broth and simmer for about 1 1/4 hours. Meanwhile prepare the coating paste. Mix grated horseradish with some lemon juice and grated lemon rind, using whole lemon. Add salt and pepper to taste, add finely chopped parsley, egg yolks, sour cream and bread crumbs. Add Worcester sauce to taste. Remove tender legs from broth, place on aluminum lined baking sheet and spread with horseradish paste. Bake for about 10 minutes.

Goose or Duck Giblets in Cream Sauce

Giblets from 1 goose or 1 duck, 1 onion, salt, 100 g (4 oz) root vegetables, peppercorn, 80 g (3 oz) butter, 50 g (1 oz) flour, 1/4 l (1/2 pint) whipping cream, ground ginger, parsley.

Chop giblets, cover with water, add salt, onion, chopped root vegetables and peppercorn. Simmer until tender. Brown 2/3 butter and flour, add part of broth and whipping cream, mix well and simmer. Rub sauce through a sieve, add finely chopped parsley, pinch of ginger and rest of the butter. Place chopped meat back into sauce, heat and serve with rice or noodles.

Duck with Mushrooms

1 duck, salt, pepper, thyme, 1 large onion, oil, 500 g (1 lb) champignons, 1/2 l (1 pint) red wine, parsley, mustard, 1/8 l (4 oz) whipping cream.

Cut duck into serving pieces, sprinkle with salt and pepper. Brown meat in hot oil on both sides, remove and place in a roasting pan. Sauté finely chopped onion and thin slices of champignons in the oil, add salt and pepper. After 5 minutes add thyme and red wine. Add this mixture to meat and roast in oven. Remove tender meat and keep warm.
Add finely chopped parsley, mustard and whipping cream to pan juices and simmer. Serve with bread dumplings.

Rabbit with Mustard

1 rabbit, salt, pepper, 2 carrots, 1 small celeriac, 3 parsnips, thyme, 1 bay leaf, 60 g (2 1/4 oz) butter, 1/10 l (2 Tbsp) white wine, 1/8 l (4 oz) whipping cream, 100 g (4 oz) mustard.

Cut rabbit into serving pieces, sprinkle with salt and pepper and rub with butter. Roast for 30 minutes, basting with hot water. In 30 minutes, spread meat with mustard, add chopped onion and vegetables. Sprinkle with thyme, add bay leaf, roast until tender. Remove meat, add wine and whipping cream to gravy and simmer. Strain gravy.

Stew Rabbit

1 rabbit, 100 g (4 oz) bacon, 1 large onion, 3 Tbsp butter, 1 bay leaf, thyme, 6 peppercorns, 6 whole allspice, piece of lemon peel, salt, 1 Tbsp flour, vinegar, sugar.

Cut rabbit into serving pieces. Brown finely chopped onion in finely chopped fried bacon, adding 1 Tbsp butter, spices, lemon peel and salt. Add rabbit, hot water and simmer. Melt rest of the butter, dust with flour and add part of rabbit broth. Mix well. Slowly add remaining rabbit broth, vinegar and sugar to taste. Stir constantly and simmer for 5 minutes. Place meat back into gravy and serve.

Rabbit Legs with Garlic

4 rabbit legs, 40 g (1 1/2 oz) bacon, 3 cloves of garlic, salt, pepper, 50 g (2 oz) lard, 2 onions, 2 Tbsp flour.

Lard legs with strips of bacon, rub with crushed garlic and sprinkle with salt and pepper. Brown finely chopped onion in lard, add legs and brown on both sides. Add a little water and simmer. Remove tender meat, dust pan juices with flour, add water and simmer. Rub gravy through a sieve.

Saddle of Venison with Champignons

500 g (1 lb) saddle of venison, salt, 80 g (3 oz) butter, 30 g (1 1/4 oz) white wine, 1/4 l (1/2 pint) sour cream, 2 Tbsp four, 200 g (8 oz) champignons, vinegar, 100 g (4 oz) carrots.

Remove membranes from venison, salt, and brown in butter on all sides. Add diced bacon, finely chopped onion and spices. Add water and simmer, basting with wine and hot water. Remove tender meat, add sour cream mixed with flour and simmer. Cook sliced champignons in water with vinegar, add diced carrots, When tender, blend into gravy. Serve with bread dumplings.

Leg of Venison in Cream Sauce

1 kg (2 lbs) leg of venison, 50 g (2 oz) bacon, salt, 1 onion, 150 g (6 oz) root vegetables, 80 g (3 oz) butter 4, peppercorns, 2 whole allspice, 2 juniper berries, 1 bay leaf, 50 g (2 oz) flour, meat bouillon, 1/4 l (1/2 pint) whipping cream, lemon, sugar and vinegar.

Remove membranes, lard with stripes of bacon and sprinkle with salt. Brown finely chopped onion and root vegetables in butter, add meat and brown on all sides. Add part of bouillon, spices and roast in oven, basting often. Remove tender meat, dust dripping with flour, add rest of the bouillon and whipping cream, strip of lemon peel and simmer. Rub sauce through a sieve, add sugar, salt and lemon juice or vinegar to taste.
Serve with bread dumplings and cranberry relish.

Meatless
Dishes

Potato Pancakes (Bramborak)

1 kg (2 lbs) potatoes, 1/2 cup milk, 2 eggs, salt, pepper, marjoram, 4 cloves of garlic, 150–200 g (7 oz) flour, lard or oil.

Peel and grate potatoes, then drain. Add hot milk, eggs, spices, crushed garlic and flour, mix well. Drop pancake batter into hot lard and fry on both sides to a golden brown. Serve immediately.

Potato Pancakes with Cracklings (Skvarky)

500 g (1lb) potatoes, 500 g (1 lb) all-purpose flour, salt, 120 g (5 oz) cracklings, 2 eggs.

Boil unpeeled potatoes until tender. Peel while warm, press through a sieve. Add salt, eggs, flour and finely chopped cracklings. Work into firm dough. Roll out dough and cut out pancakes. Place pancakes on greased baking sheet and bake in oven to a golden brown.
Serve with spinach or other vegetables.

Potato Pizza

2 kg (4 lbs) potatoes, 6 egg yolks, 2 containers sour cream, salt, pepper, sweet paprika, marjoram, 3 cloves of garlic, 2 red and 2 green bell peppers, 100 g (4 oz) bacon, shortening.

Peel raw potatoes, grate coarsely. Mix with egg yolks, sour cream and spices. Slice bell peppers into small strips, add to potato mixture. Place potato dough on greased baking sheet, cover with thin slices of bacon and bake in preheated oven for about 60 minutes.

Potato Mush (Skubanky)

1 kg (2 lbs) potatoes, peeled and quartered, 200 g (8 oz) all-purpose flour, 100 g (4 oz) lard.

Pour hot water over potatoes, cook until done. Drain, reserving the water. Mash potatoes until smooth. Make wells in potatoes with the handle of a wooden spoon, fill with flour. Cover with half the reserved water, put on the lid and leave for about 10 minutes, Drain water from potatoes and mix again into smooth dough. Dip large spoon in hot lard and scoop out mixture by spoonfuls on a plate. Sprinkle with ground poppy seeds, sugar and drizzle with melted butter. If you like you can also fry skubanky in lard until golden brown.

Mushroom Pudding

300 g (12 oz) fresh mushrooms, 100 g (4 oz) butter, 3 rolls, milk, 3 eggs, salt, 2 cloves of garlic, pepper, 20 g (3/4 oz) semolina.

Slice cleaned mushrooms and sauté in butter. Slice rolls and drizzle with milk. Mix soft butter, beaten eggs, squeezed rolls, mushrooms, crushed garlic, salt and pepper in a bowl, add semolina. Fill greased casserole with mixture, drizzle with melted butter and bake in oven until golden brown.

Mushroom Pudding with Barley, "Kuba"

300 g (12 oz) barley, 50 g (2 oz) dried mushrooms, 1 onion, 3 cloves of garlic, marjoram, salt, pepper, 30 g (1 1/4 oz) lard, 30 g (1 1/4 oz) butter.

Soak dried mushrooms in cold water for 1 hour. Rinse barley, cook in salted water until tender. Brown finely chopped onion in lard, add squeezed chopped mushrooms, simmer. Mix soft mushrooms with barley, add crushed garlic, salt, marjoram and pepper to taste. Fill well greased casserole with mixture, drizzle with melted butter and bake in oven for about 30 minute.
Serve with sweet / sour gherkins.

Breaded Champignons

250 g (8 oz) champignons, 2 eggs, flour, bread crumbs, salt, pepper, oil.

Brush champignons under running water, dry. If champignon is too large cut in half. Sprinkle with salt, dip in flour, then eggs, then breadcrumbs. Fry in hot oil until golden brown. Serve with potatoes, garlic butter and slices of lemon.

Sautéed Mushrooms with Eggs

500 g (1 lb) fresh mushrooms, 50 g (2 oz) butter, 1 onion, salt, pepper, caraway seeds, 4 eggs.

Clean and slice mushrooms. Brown finely chopped onion in butter, add mushrooms, caraway seeds, salt and pepper. Sauté, add beaten egg, mix until eggs are set. Serve with bread.

Cheese Dumplings

1/4 l (1/2 pint) milk, 60 g (2 1/4 oz) all-purpose flour, salt, sweet paprika, nutmeg, 200 g (8 oz) emental cheese (Swiss), 4 eggs, oil.

Thicken warm milk with flour, cool. Add salt, sweet paprika and nutmeg. Cut cheese in cubes, add to milk and eggs. Mix well. Scoop out mixture by spoonfuls and fry in hot oil to a golden brown.
Serve with vegetable salad.

Meatless
Dishes

Roquefort Patties

200 g (8 oz) roquefort cheese, 3 Tbsp. breadcrumbs, 3 Tbsp. milk, salt, pepper, Worcester sauce, 50 g (2 oz) butter, 2 eggs, oil.

Mix soft butter with salt. Soak bread crumbs with milk. Finely grate cheese and mix with butter and breadcrumbs. Add eggs, pepper and a couple of drops of Worcester sauce.

Add more breadcrumbs as needed. Form flat patties, brown in hot oil to a golden brown.
Serve with mashed potatoes.

Prune Pockets

600 g (20 oz) potatoes, salt, pepper, 1 egg, 60 g (2 1/4 oz) semolina, 200 g (8 oz) all-purpose flour, prune cheese, sugar, grated cottage cheese, butter.

Cook unpeeled potatoes, cool, peel and grate finely. Add flour, semolina, salt and egg. Work into firm dough. Roll out thin sheet, cut into 3-inch squares. Place 1 Tbsp. prune cheese in center of each square and fold over into a triangle, seal the edges. Boil in salted water for about 3 minutes, lifting them gently from the bottom. Boil for 7 minutes longer. Drain and dry. Sprinkle with finely grated cheese, sugar and drizzle with melted butter.

Hard Curd Cheese for Grating

Because the above product is not available in most foreign countries, here is how to prepare it yourselves. Get 1 package of high percentage cheese (Cottage). Place in a pot, warm slowly, stirring constantly for several minutes. Drain. Place in cheese cloth and squeeze well. Place in refrigerator for 1 hour. Grate and use with all kinds of fruit dumplings.

Fried Dumplings with Eggs

8 slices of bread dumplings, 1 onion, 40 g (1 1/2 oz) butter, 4 eggs, salt, pepper.

Dice bread dumplings, brown finely chopped onion in butter, add dumplings and brown on all sides. Cover with beaten eggs, salt and pepper, stir until eggs are set.
Serve with sweet-sour gherkins.

Assorted Dumplings

Bread Dumplings I

2 rolls, 30 g (1 1/4 oz) butter, 400 g (14 oz) all-purpose flour, 3/4 package baking powder, 1 egg, salt, 4 Tbsp. milk or water.

Brown diced rolls in butter. Sift flour into a bowl with baking powder. Add egg, salt and milk or water. Work into smooth dough, add browned roll cubes. Leave for 5 minutes. With wet hands shape dough into 2 rolls, put dumplings in boiling salted water, making sure they do not stick to bottom. Boil gently for about 20 minutes, turning after 10 minutes. Remove dumplings from pan, slice with electric knife or thread.

Bread Dumplings II

6 stale rolls, 120 g (5 oz) semolina, 100 g (4 oz) flour, 1/4 l (1/2 pint) milk, 2 eggs, 40 g (1 1/2 oz) butter, salt.

Blend semolina, flour, milk, egg, salt and melted butter with electric mixer. Add diced rolls. Let this thin dough stand for about 30 minutes. With wet hands shape dough into 2 rolls, put dumplings in boiling salted water. Boil for about 30 minutes, turning once after 15 minutes. Remove dumplings and leave to rest for several minutes. Slice with electric knife or strong thread.

Dumpling Boiled in a Napkin

300 g (12 oz) stale rolls, 30 g (1 1/4 oz) butter, 300 g (12 oz) flour, 3 eggs, salt, 1/4 l (1/2 pint) milk.

Dice rolls and brown in butter. Mix flour with salted milk and beaten egg yolk, add browned diced rolls. Fold in stiffly beaten egg whites. Form dough into roll, place on wet, buttered napkin. Roll and tic both ends loosely. Cover and gently boil for about 1 hour. Remove dumpling from napkin and slice with a thread.

Assorted
Dumplings

Potato Dumplings

600 g (20 oz) potatoes, salt, 100 g (4 oz) semolina, 1 egg, 100 g (4 oz) all-purpose flour.

Boil unpeeled potatoes, peel while still warm and grate. Add flour, semolina, salt, egg and pinch of baking powder. Knead well, form 2 rolls about 3 inches in diameter, boil gently in salted water for about 15–20 minutes, turning several times with care. Remove from boiling water and slice with a thread.

Potato Dumplings with Bread

500 g (1 lb) potatoes, 80 g (3 oz) semolina, 70 g (2 1/2 oz) potato flour, 3 egg yolks, 1 tsp. salt, pinch of baking powder, 10 g (1 Tbsp) butter, 2 rolls.

Boil unpeeled potatoes, drain, peel and grate while still warm. Add semolina, potato flour, egg yolks, baking powder and salt. Knead into firm dough. Add diced rolls browned in butter. Form 2 rolls about 3 inches in diameter and boil in salted water. Make sure dumplings do not stick to the bottom of the pan. Boil for about 18 minutes, turning several times. Remove from water and slice with a thread.

Dumplings with Bacon

6 stale rolls, 100 g (4 oz) bacon or cooked smoked meat, 1/4 l (1/2 pint) milk, 2 egg yolks, 50 g (2 oz) all-purpose flour, 2 Tbsp. butter, salt.

Assorted Dumplings

Mix milk, egg yolks, salt and flour into a dough. Leave for a few minutes. Brown finely chopped bacon, add diced rolls browned in butter. Add this mixture to dough and form small round dumplings. Boil in salted water for about 10–15 minutes. Serve sprinkled with fried bacon and its fat and Sauerkraut.

Raised Dumplings

For yeast: 10 g (1/2 oz) compressed yeast, 10 g (1/2 oz) sugar,
1/16 l (2 oz) milk, 2 Tbsp. flour.

For dough: 500 g (1 lb) flour, 2 eggs, 1 egg yolk, 40 g (1 1/2 oz) sugar, salt,
1 tsp. grated lemon rind, 100 g (4 oz) butter, 1/8 l (4 oz) milk.

For topping: 150 g (6 oz) butter, 50 g (2 oz) ground poppy seeds,
30 g (1 1/4 oz) powder sugar, 450 g (16 oz) prune cheese.

Crumble yeast in warm milk with sugar. Mix well, add flour,
cover and leave to rise in a warm place. Sift flour into a large
bowl, add eggs, egg yolk, sugar, pinch of salt, lemon rind and
butter. Pour in yeast mixture and warm milk. Beat into a
firm dough, dust top with flour, cover with a clean napkin
and leave to rise. When dough doubles in bulk, place on
floured board and knead gently. Form rolls, cover with
napkin and leave to rise for 10 more minutes, then slice and
form round dumplings. Place individual dumplings on
floured board, cover and leave to rise. Place in boiling salted
water, cover and cook for about 20 minutes. Remove from
pot and tear open with 2 forks.
Serve with ground poppy seeds, powder sugar melted butter
and prune cheese.

Raised Dumplings with Blueberries

10 g (1/2 oz) compressed yeast, 1 tsp. sugar, 1/4 l (1/2 pint) milk,
500 g (1 lb) all-purpose flour, pinch of salt, blueberries, grated cottage
cheese, sugar, butter, 1 egg.

Mix yeast and sugar in warm milk. Leave to rise. Sift flour
into bowl, add egg, pinch of salt. Pour in yeast mixture and
remaining warm milk, work into a firm dough, cover with a
napkin and leave to rise for about 1 hour. Cut into uniform
pieces, stretch to make squares, fill with fruit and form
round dumplings. Cover with napkin on floured board and
leave to rise for 15 minutes. Boil in salted water, cover after
4 minutes. Remove lid when dumplings rise to the surface,
turn them over and boil for 4 more minutes uncovered.

Assorted
Dumplings

Remove dumplings, prick each with fork to let steam out.
Serve with sugar, grated cottage cheese and melted butter.

Cottage Cheese Dough Fruit Dumplings

200 g (8 oz) cottage cheese, 50 g (2 oz) butter, pinch of salt, 1 egg,
1/4 l (1/2 pint) milk, 500 g (1 lb) all-purpose flour, about
500 g (1/2 pint) cherries, apricots or strawberries, powder sugar, grated
cottage cheese, butter.

Cream butter with egg and salt. Add cottage cheese, milk and
flour, knead into a dough. Form roll and slice. Fill each slice
with fruit, seal well and form round dumplings. Boil in salted
water for about 5–8 minutes.
Serve with sugar, grated cottage cheese and melted butter.

Scalded Dough Dumplings

1/2 l (1 pint) milk, 100 g (4 oz) butter, pinch of salt, 350 g (12 oz) all-
purpose flour, 4 eggs, 500 g (1 lb) plums or apricots, grated cottage
cheese, sugar, butter.

Bring milk and butter to a boil. Pour in flour slowly, stirring
constantly till dough doesn't stick to the pot. Cool, blend in
eggs, mix well. Roll out dough on floured board, cut squares,
fill with fruit with stones, because it forms only a thin layer.
Boil dumplings in salted water for about 5–8 minutes.
Serve with sugar, grated cheese and melted butter.

Potato Prune Dumplings

2 large cooked potatoes, 250 g (8 oz) all-purpose flour, 1 egg, salt,
1/16 l (2 oz) milk, prunes or plums grated cottage cheese, sugar, butter.

Finely grate cooked peeled potatoes, add flour, egg, pinch of
salt and milk. Work into a stiff dough. Form thin roll and
slice. Fill centers with 1 prune or plum, form into dumplings
and boil in salted water for about 7 minutes.
Sprinkle with sugar, grated cheese, drizzle and butter.

Fancy Desserts, Cakes and Holiday Treats

Old Bohemian Easter Cake (Mazanec)

500 g (1 lb) all-purpose flour, 120 g (5 oz) butter, 100 g (4 oz) sugar,
3 egg yolks, 35 g (1 1/2 oz) yeast, 1/4 l (1/2 pint) milk, salt,
30 g (1 1/4 oz) almonds, 40 g (1 1/2 oz) raisins, 1 vanilla sugar, grated
lemon peel, 1 Tbsp rum, 1 egg for brushing.

Add yeast and 1 tsp. sugar to part of warm milk and leave to
rise. In large bowl mix flour, sugar, pinch of salt, lemon peel,
vanilla sugar and rum. Pour in yeast mixture with warm
milk, melted butter and beaten egg yolks. Knead into a
dough. Place dough on floured board and add cleaned
raisins and blanched, chopped almonds. Place in large bowl,
cover with napkin and leave to rise for about 1 hour. Form
round cake, put on well greased baking sheet, brush top with
egg. With sharp knife cut a cross on top, sprinkle with
chopped almonds. Bake in preheated oven slowly for about
60 minutes.

"Easter Lamb"

125 g (5 oz) butter, 2 Tbsp. honey, 125 g (5 oz) sugar, 3 egg yolks, 1 vanilla
sugar, 20 g (3/4 oz) yeast, salt, 1 cup of milk, 350 g (12 oz) all purpose flour,
50 g (2 oz) raisins, 50 g (2 oz) almonds, butter, breadcrumbs.

Blend yeast and 1 tsp. flour with part of warm milk. Leave to
rise. Cream soft butter with honey, sugar and egg yolks. Add
pinch of salt, vanilla sugar and yeast mixture. Add flour and
milk. Blend in raisins and blanched, chopped almonds.
Grease both halves of lamb form well and sprinkle with
breadcrumbs. Fill one half with dough and rise to leave for
about 1 hour. Cover with other half of the form and bake
slowly, turning once. Sprinkle baked lamb with sugar, make
eyes out of raisins and tie a ribbon around his neck.

Real Bohemian Stuffed "Buchty"

20 g (3/4 oz) yeast, 50 g (2 oz) sugar, 1/4 l (1/2 pint) milk,
500 g (1 lb.) flour, 1 vanilla sugar, salt, grated rind from 1 lemon, 2 egg
yolks, 50 g (2 oz) butter, 100 g (4 oz) butter for brushing, powder sugar.

Blend crumbled yeast with 1 Tbsp. sugar, 1 Tbsp. flour and
2 Tbsp. warm milk. Leave to rise. Sift flour into large bowl,
add sugar, pinch of salt and lemon rind. Pour in yeast
mixture, warm milk and beaten egg yolks. Blend in melted
butter. Mix dough well until little bubbles form. Cover with
napkin and leave to rise for about 1 hour in a warm place.
Roll out dough on well-floured board and cut into squares.
Fill centers with filling mixture, bring edges of dough
together and seal well. Place on a well-greased pan seam
down. Brush each "Buchta" with melted butter and leave to
rise again for about 1/2 hour. Brush once more with melted
butter and place in a preheated oven, bake for about
45 minutes until light brown. Remove from pan, cool, separate and sprinkle with sugar.

Prune Filling: 200 g (8 oz) prune cheese, grated lemon rind, 1 vanilla sugar,
1 tsp. rum.

Warm prune cheese with a little water. Add lemon rind,
vanilla sugar and rum.

Poppy Seed Filling: 150g (6 oz) poppy seeds, 1/4 l (1/2 pint) milk,
80 g (3 oz) sugar, 20 g (3/4 oz) butter, grated lemon rind, 1 tsp. rum.

ground poppy seeds mix with milk, sugar and butter.
Simmer, stirring constantly. Add lemon rind and rum to
taste.

Cottage Cheese Filling: 300 g (11 oz) cottage cheese, 30 g (1 1/4 oz) butter,
2 egg yolks, 50 g (2 oz) sugar, 1 vanilla sugar, 2 Tbsp. milk,
20 g (3/4 oz) raisins, 2 egg whites.

Cream butter with egg yolks and sugar. Add cottage cheese
and milk. Fold in stiff egg whites and raisins.

Poppy Seed "Babovka"

120 g (5 oz) butter, 140 g (5 1/2 oz) sugar, egg yolks, salt, grated lemon rind, 30 g (1 1/4 oz) yeast, 1/4 l (1/2 pint) milk, 500 g (1 lb) all-purpose flour, 50g (2 oz) almonds.

Filling: 120 g (5 oz) ground poppy seeds, 1 cup milk, 50 g (2 oz) sugar, pinch of cinnamon and vanilla sugar, 20 g (3/4 oz) butter.

Cream butter with sugar, add egg yolk and whip into a foam. Add pinch of salt, grated lemon rind and yeast mixture, which we prepared first. We mixed yeast with 1 tsp. sugar, 2 Tbsp. warm milk and 1 tsp. flour and left to rise. Add warm milk alternately with flour. Knead dough well, cover with a napkin and leave to rise for about 1 hour. Meanwhile mix poppy seeds with milk, sugar, cinnamon, vanilla sugar and butter. Simmer, stirring constantly. Grease form well and sprinkle with breadcrumbs, sprinkle bottom with chopped almonds. Fill form half way with dough, spread with poppy seed filling, cover with remaining dough. Leave to rise for about 30 minutes. Brush with melted butter and bake for about 50 minutes. Sprinkle baked, "Babovka" with sugar.

Fine "Babovka"

125 g (5 oz) butter, 240 g (8 oz) sugar, grated lemon rind, 1/4 l (1/2 pint) whipping cream, 5 egg yolks, 420 g (15 oz) all purpose flour, 5 egg whites, 1 packet baking powder, 60 g (2 1/4 oz) chocolate or 1 Tbsp. cocoa, 1 Tbsp. lemon juice.

Beat butter until smooth, gradually adding sugar, egg yolks and lemon juice. Add to mixture, alternating half of the flour and all of the whipping cream. Mix remaining flour with baking powder. Beat egg whites until stiff and alternating egg whites and flour, lightly mix into the dough. Divide dough into 3 equal parts. Grease a special "Babovka" form and sprinkle with fine breadcrumbs. Put 1/3 of the dough in the form. Add chocolate or cocoa to the second part of the dough and pour over the first part. Cover with third part of the dough. Bake for about 1 hour. Sprinkle cooled "Babovka" with powder sugar.

Fancy Desserts, Cakes and Holiday Treats

Pancakes (Livance)

250 g (8 oz) flour, 1/2 l (1 pint) milk, 15 g (3/4 oz) yeast,
30 g (1 1/4 oz) sugar, salt, grated lemon rind, 1 egg, fruit jam,
grated farmer cheese.

Crumble yeast in part of warm milk add 1 tsp. sugar and
some flour, leave to rise. Add pinch of salt, lemon rind, egg
and remaining sugar. Mix in milk alternating with flour.
Cover with a napkin and leave to rise for 30 minutes. Fry on
a greased pan on both sides. Spread with jam, sprinkle with
grated cheese and roll up or fold.

Bohemian Doughnuts (Vdolky)

500 g (1 lb) all purpose flour, 50 g (2 oz) sugar, 1/4 l (1/2 pint) milk,
20 g (3/4 oz) yeast, salt, 1 egg yolk, 50 g (2 oz) butter, oil, jam or prune
cheese, cottage cheese, 1 cup sour cream.

Blend yeast in half of warm milk, add 1 tsp. sugar and 1 tsp.
flour, leave to rise. Place flour in bowl, add pinch of salt and
sugar, pour in yeast mixture and remaining milk with beaten
egg yolk. Add melted butter. Mix into a smooth dough and
leave to rise for about 1 hour. Roll out dough about 1/2 inch
thick, cut out circles, place on floured board and leave to
rise again, turning once. Place dough circles in hot oil, cover
for about 3 minutes, frying one side and uncover when frying
the other side. Spread fried doughnuts with prune cheese or
other jam, sprinkle with grated cheese and cover with sour
cream.

Baked Crepes

DOUGH: 100 g (4 oz) flour, 1/4 l (1/2 pint) milk, pinch of salt, 4 eggs,
50 g (2 oz) butter, 60 g (2 1/4 oz) butter for frying.

FILLING: 350 g (12 oz) cottage cheese, 70 g (2 1/2 oz) sugar, 2 egg yolks,
1 tsp. lemon rind, 1 vanilla sugar, pinch of salt.

TO BAKE: 200 g (8 oz) sour cream, 1 egg, 50 g (2 oz) powder sugar

Mix flour with milk, add pinch of salt, let stand for
30 minutes. Then add sugar and beaten eggs. To make filling
blend cottage cheese with egg yolks, vanilla sugar, sugar,
grated lemon rind and pinch of salt. Heat a frying pan, brush
with butter and gradually fry 6 crepes. Spread with filling,
fold edges lightly and roll up. Place in a well greased Pyrex
dish and cover with sour cream mixed with egg and sugar.
Bake in preheated oven for about 15 minutes. Serve hot,
sprinkled with powder sugar.

Bohemian Cakes (Kolacky)

DOUGH: 1 kg (2 lbs) flour, 2 packages dried yeast, salt, 1/2 lemon,
80 g sugar, 150 g (6 oz) butter, 1 Tbsp rum, 1/2 l (1 pint) milk.

POPPY SEED FILLING: 65 g (2-1/2 oz) ground poppy seeds, 1/8 l (4 oz) milk,
1 Tbsp sugar, 1/2 tsp cocoa, pinch of cinnamon, pinch of ground cloves.

COTTAGE CHEESE FILLING: 125 g (5 oz) dry cottage cheese, 2 Tbsp. sugar,
1 egg yolk, 1/2 vanilla pod, 1/2 lemon, pinch of nutmeg,
20 g (3/4 oz) raisins.

PRUNE FILLING: 4 Tbsp prune cheese, 1 Tbsp rum, and 1/2 lemon

DOUGH: Blend flour with dried yeast, pinch of salt, grated
lemon rind, sugar and scraped inside of vanilla pod. Add egg
yolks, soft butter, rum and warm milk. Mix well with electric
beater. Cover dough with a napkin and leave to rise for
about 30 minutes in a warm place.

POPPY SEED FILLING: Blend ground poppy seeds with
milk, sugar, cocoa, cinnamon and ground cloves and simmer
for about 5 minutes, stirring constantly. Cool.

COTTAGE CHEESE FILLING: Cream cottage cheese with
sugar, egg yolk, scraped inside of 1/2 vanilla pod, grated
lemon rind, nutmeg and raisins.

PRUNE FILLING: Mix prune cheese with rum until smooth,
add grated lemon rind to taste.

Cut dough in half, roll out each part on floured board, cut into small squares about 3 x 3 inches. Fill each square with 1 tsp. of one of the above fillings. Join opposite corners of the dough to close in filling. Place on greased baking sheet and leave to rise for 15 minutes. Brush with beaten egg and bake for about 35 minutes. Following cakes will need only about 25 minutes.

Raised Poppy Seed or Nut Roll

DOUGH: 500 g (1 lb) flour, 20 g (3/4 oz) yeast, 1Tbsp sugar, 1 egg, 125 g (5 oz) soft butter, 1 tsp salt, 2/10 l (4 Tbsp) sour cream.

POPPY SEED FILLING: 200 g (8 oz) sugar, 150 g (6 oz) ground poppy seeds, 75 ml (1/8 pint) milk, 1 tsp. grated lemon rind, 50 g (2 oz) raisins, 75 g (3 oz) breadcrumbs, 1 egg.

NUT FILLING: 175 g (7 oz) sugar, 150 g (6 oz) ground nuts, 50 ml (3 Tbsp) milk, pinch of ground cloves, 1/2 tsp. cinnamon, juice of 1/2 lemon, 75 g (3 oz) breadcrumbs.

Blend yeast and sugar in 3 tbsp. water. Add to flour together with egg, butter, pinch of salt and sour cream.
Work into dough, leave to rise for 1-1/2 hours.

POPPY SEED FILLING: Boil sugar with 3 Tbsp. water until syrupy. Add poppy seeds, milk and lemon rind, simmer, stirring constantly. Cool. Blend in breadcrumbs.

NUT FILLING: Boil sugar with 3 Tbsp. water until syrupy. Add nuts, milk and ground cloves, cinnamon and lemon rind. Cool, add breadcrumbs. Knead dough again, roll out on floured board. Spread dough with either poppy seed or nut filling. Roll sheet from longer end into a roll, set on well-greased baking sheet and leave to rise again. Brush top with beaten egg and bake for about 50 minutes.

Special Little Wedding Cakes

500 g (1 lb) flour, 1/4 l (1/2 pint) milk, 30 g (1 1/4 oz) yeast,
80 g (3 oz) sugar, 1 vanilla sugar, salt, 3 egg yolks, lemon rind,
100 g (4 oz) butter

Use fillings same as for stuffed "Buchty" (Poppy Seed, Cottage Cheese or Prune Cheese). Mix yeast with 1/3 warm milk, 1 tsp. sugar and leave to rise. Place flour in large bowl, add pinch of salt, sugar, yeast mixture and remaining milk with beaten yolks. Add grated lemon rind and work into a smooth dough, cover and leave to rise. Form small balls, place on well-greased baking sheet. Make indentations in the centers with bottom of floured glass and fill with Poppy Seed, Cottage Cheese or Prune Butter, brush edges with beaten egg. Leave to rise. Bake in preheated oven for about 30 minutes. Sprinkle with sugar.

Large "Domazlice" Cakes

Prepare dough as for wedding cakes. Form two large round cakes with raised edges. Place on greased baking sheet. Fill cakes alternating Poppy Seed, Cottage Cheese and Prune Cheese fillings. Decorate Cottage Cheese filling with raisins, Poppy Seed and Prune Cheese filling with peeled almond halves. Brush edges with beaten egg. Bake in preheated oven for about 40 minutes.
Cool and cut cakes into 8 wedges.

Apple Strudel

350 g (12 oz) flour, pinch of salt, 1/8 l (4 oz) lukewarm water, 3 drops vinegar, 1 egg, 20 g (3/4 oz) lard, 60 g (2 1/4 oz) butter (melted), 750 g (1 1/2 lbs) semi tart apples, 100 g (4 oz) bread crumbs, 2 Tbsp. butter, 60 g (2 1/4 oz) sugar, cinnamon, 1 Tbsp. rum, 30 g (1 1/4 oz) raisins, 20 g (3/4 oz) coarsely chopped almonds, grated lemon rind.

Sift flour on pastry board. Blend beaten egg in lukewarm water with salt, melted lard and vinegar. Pour slowly into a

Fancy Desserts,
Cakes and
Holiday Treats

well in the middle of the flour. Mix into a thin dough, using a knife, knead dough until smooth and elastic. Divide into two parts, roll out first part on floured kitchen towel, slide hands under dough and with the backs of your clenched fists stretch dough until very thin, cut off thick edges. Brush prepared dough with melted butter and sprinkle with breadcrumbs browned in butter. Spread with pared and thinly sliced apples; sprinkle with sugar, raisins, cinnamon, almonds and lemon rind, drizzle with rum. Using the kitchen towel roll up Strudel onto a greased baking sheet and brush with melted butter. Prepare second Strudel the same way. Bake for about 40 minutes, brushing top with melted butter several times. Dust with sugar and slice to serve.

Cherry Strudel

250 g (8 oz) flour, pinch of salt, 1 egg, 1 Tbsp. oil, 1/8 l (4 oz) lukewarm water, 150 g (6 oz) bread crumbs, 100g (4 oz) melted butter, 1 kg (2 lbs) pitted cherries.

Mix flour, salt, egg, oil and water and knead into smooth dough. Place in plastic bag and leave to rest for 1/2 hour. Use half the butter to brown breadcrumbs. Roll out dough on floured pastry board, use both hands to stretch thin, and place on a large floured cloth. Brush with melted butter, sprinkle with browned breadcrumbs and cover with cherries. Roll strudel from the cloth onto a greased baking sheet. Brush with butter and bake for about 40 minutes. Dust with powder sugar.

Apple Cake Without Flour

6 eggs, 250 g (8 oz) sugar, 75 g (3 oz) semolina, 1 Tbsp. cocoa, 250 g (8 oz) grated apples, 120 g (4 3/4 oz) ground hazelnuts, apricot jam, 200 g (8 oz) chocolate for icing, a few whole hazelnuts.

Beat egg yolks with 1/2 sugar until smooth, add semolina, cocoa, apples and ground nuts. Beat egg whites until stiff. Fold in rest of sugar and add to dough. Pour into a greased cake form and bake for about 50 minutes. When done spread cake wit apricot jam thinned with water. Leave to cool. Spread cake with melted chocolate and decorate with whole hazelnuts.

Currant Upsidedown Cake

250 g (8 oz) butter, 175 g (7 oz) sugar, pinch of salt, 4 eggs, grated lemon rind of 1 lemon, 200 g (8 oz) flour, 2 tsp. baking powder, 750 g (1 1/2 lbs) red currant, 150 g (6 oz) currant jelly.

Cream soft butter with salt and sugar. Gradually add eggs. Blend in flour mixed with lemon rind and baking powder. Line bottom of cake form with aluminium foil, slide in cake form and close. Fold overlapping foil up and press firmly on the form to prevent currant juice leaking out while baking. Grease sides and bottom of form with butter. Spread bottom evenly with clean red currants, pour in dough and smooth over. Bake in preheated oven for about 1 hour. When done loosen edges of cake with knife. Turn upside down, remove cake form and aluminium foil. Spread top of cake with melted currant jelly and serve with whipped cream.

Chocolate Cake

100 g (4 oz) raisins, 2 small glasses of rum, 100 g (4 oz) milk chocolate, 100 g (4 oz) bitter chocolate, 125 g (5 oz) whipping cream, 100 g (4 oz) butter, 6 eggs, 100 g (4 oz) sugar, 200 g (8 oz) ground almonds, 200 g (8 oz) grated biscuits, cinnamon, 100 g (4 oz) chocolate frosting, pralines for decoration.

Soak raisins in rum. Break up chocolate and together with whipping cream, melt over steam (set over a pot of boiling water), stirring constantly. Add butter. Let chocolate mixture cool for about 10 minutes. Then add egg yolks, sugar, almonds, grated biscuits, cinnamon and drained raisins. Beat egg whites until stiff and fold gently into chocolate dough. Pour dough into well-greased form and bake for about 60 minutes, leave to cool. Spread with chocolate frosting and decorate with pralines.

Fancy Desserts, Cakes and Holiday Treats

Blueberry Cake

DOUGH: 125 g (5 oz) butter, grated rind of 1/2 lemon, 125 g (5 oz) sugar, 2 eggs, 250 g (8 oz) flour, 1 tsp. baking powder, 1 tsp. rum, 500 g (1 lb) blueberries.

FROSTING: 1/4 l (1/2 pint) milk, pinch of salt, 1 Tbsp. butter, 2 Tbsp. sugar, 20 g (3/4 oz) semolina, 2 eggs, grated rind of 1/2 lemon, 100 g (4 oz) ground almonds.

Mix above ingredients into a dough, adding rum last. Pour into greased cake form. Bake in preheated over for about 30 minutes. Bring to boil milk, salt, butter and sugar. While stirring constantly add semolina, simmer shortly. Blend in egg yolks mixed with lemon rind and almonds.
Gently fold in stiffly beaten egg whites. Cover pre-baked cake with blueberries and spread with semolina mixture. Bake for 30 more minutes. Sprinkle with powder sugar.

Apricot Cake

DOUGH: 125 g (5 oz) butter, grated lemon rind, 175 g (6 oz) sugar, 3 eggs, 225 g (8 oz) flour, pinch of baking powder, 1 Tbsp. rum

FILLING: 200 g (8 oz) ricotta cheese, (20 % fat) grated lemon rind, 100 g (4 oz) sugar, 100 g (4 oz) ground almonds, 400 g (14 oz) apricots

TOPPING: 100 g (4 oz) flour, 60 g (2 1/4 oz) butter, 80 g (3 1/4 oz) sugar, pinch of cinnamon.

Mix above ingredients, adding rum last. Pour dough into greased cake form. Bake in preheated oven for about 20 minutes. Blend cheese, egg yolk, lemon rind, sugar and almonds. Soak apricots in hot water shortly. Peel, remove stones and chop finely. Add to cheese filling together with stiffly beaten egg whites. Spread pre-baked cake with apricot mixture and sprinkle with topping made from above ingredients. Bake for 40 more minutes.

Hazelnut Cake

8 eggs, 200 g (8 oz) sugar, grated lemon rind from 1/2 lemon, 2 Tbsp. lemon juice, 250 g (8 oz) ground hazelnuts, 2 Tbsp. flour, 20 g (3/4 oz) butter, 1/2 l (1 pint) whipping cream, 2 packages vanilla sugar, browned sliced almonds.

Cream egg yolks with sugar until smooth. Add lemon rind, lemon juice, nuts and flour. Fold in stiffly beaten egg whites. Pour into well-greased cake tin, bake for about 60 minutes. When cake is cool split into 2 layers. Fill with half of the whipped cream with vanilla sugar, cover with remaining whipped cream and decorate with sliced almonds.

Rum Bomb

4 eggs, 100 g (4 oz) sugar, 80 g (3 oz) flour, 40 g (1 1/2 oz) potato flour, 3 Tbsp. cocoa, 1 tsp. baking powder, 5 Tbsp. rum, 250 g (8 oz) whipping cream, 200 g (8 oz) chocolate frosting.

Beat egg whites with 4 Tbsp. of cold water, gradually add 80 g (3 oz) sugar and beat mixture until stiff. Gradually add egg yolks, sift in flour, add potato flour, 2 Tbsp. cocoa and baking powder. Mix lightly, pour dough into greased round oven-proof bowl. Bake for about 40–50 minutes. Slice cooked cake twice into layers, drizzle cake rounds with 4 Tbsp. rum. Whip cream with remaining sugar, add remaining rum and cocoa. Spread bottom round with half of whipped cream, cover with second round and spread with remaining whipped cream, cover with third part of cake. Spread cake with chocolate frosting.

Sponge Rum Fruit Roll

4 eggs, 170 g (6 1/2 oz) sugar, 1 tsp. grated lemon rind, 150 g (6 oz) flour, 1 tsp. baking powder, 1 Tbsp. cocoa, 1–2 cups fruit of your choice soaked in rum marinade, 1/2 l (1 pint) whipping cream.

Beat eggs with 4 Tbsp. warm water until foamy. Add 150 g (6 oz) sugar and lemon rind. Whip until egg mixture is creamy white. Spread dough on baking sheet covered with wax paper. Bake for about 10 minutes at 200 °C (325 °F). Turn sponge cake sheet onto clean cloth sprinkled with sugar, cover with damp cloth and cool. Peel off wax paper. Finely chop rum soaked fruit. Whip cream with remaining sugar. Mix fruit and rum marinade with half the whipped cream, spread on sponge cake sheet and roll, using the cloth. Spread finished roll with remaining whipped cream and decorate with rum fruit.

Karlsbad Cake

250 g (8 oz) soft butter, 250 g (8 oz) sugar, 250 g (8 oz) bitter chocolate, 4 egg whites, 100 g (4 oz) ground hazelnuts, 1 vanilla sugar, 6 large Karlsbad Waffles, 150 g (6 oz) powder sugar.

Cream butter with 1/2 of sugar until smooth. Break up 150 g (6 oz) chocolate and melt over steam. Beat egg whites until stiff, gradually adding remaining sugar. Mix butter mixture gently into warm chocolate. Add nuts and vanilla sugar, fold in stiff egg whites. Place 1 waffle on cake plate, spread with chocolate cream, cover with another waffle, spread again and continue until all waffles are used, spreading top with last of the chocolate cream. Add powder sugar and 2–3 Tbsp. lukewarm water to remaining chocolate. Spread this chocolate mixture over top and sides of the cake. Chill for several hours before serving.

Punch Strips

DOUGH: 4 eggs, 125 g (5 oz) sugar, 1 vanilla sugar, 125 g (5 oz) flour, 1 tsp baking powder.

FILLING: 225 g (8 oz) grated biscuits, 100 g (4 oz) browned ground hazelnuts, 100 g (4 oz) ground almonds, 1/10 l (2 Tbsp) cherry liquor, 1/10 l (2 Tbsp) white wine, 1/10 l (2 Tbsp) rum, 3 Tbsp cocoa, 100 g (4 oz) sugar, 2 Tbsp lemon juice, 1/2 cup currant jelly.

SPREAD: 1/2 cup red currant jelly.

DECORATION: 250 g (8 oz) powder sugar, 2–3 Tbsp. lemon juice, Marachino cherries.

Beat eggs until foamy, add sugar and vanilla sugar. Add flour mixed with baking powder. Spread dough on baking sheet covered with wax paper, bake for 12 minutes. Cut cooled cake into 2 thin layers, remove wax paper. Make filling from above ingredients. Spread both layers with jelly. Spread one with filling, cover with the second and press together lightly. Mix powder sugar with lemon juice and spread on top of cake. Decorate with cherries and slice into small strips.

Punch Cake

DOUGH: 200 g (8 oz) sugar, 10 eggs, 1 vanilla sugar, grated rind of 1/2 lemon, 220 g (8 oz) all-purpose flour, 20 g (3/4 oz) butter and 20 g (3/4 oz) flour for both forms, few drops red food colouring, 30 g (1 1/4 oz) bitter chocolate, red currant jelly for spread.

PUNCH MIXTURE: 120 g (5 oz) sugar, 1/8 l (4 oz) water 160 g (6 oz) red currant jelly, juice of 1 lemon and 1 orange, 1/16 l (2 oz) rum, 1/16 l (2 oz) white wine.

FROSTING: 300 g (11 oz) powder sugar, 1 Tbsp. hot water, 2 drops red food colouring, punch as needed.

Cream egg yolk, grated lemon rind and vanilla sugar for 20 minutes. Fold in stiff beaten egg whites and flour. Divide dough in half. Place first half into cake form greased with

Fancy Desserts, Cakes and Holiday Treats

butter and sprinkled with flour. Bake. Divide second half into 3 parts. Leave one third of dough light, mix a few drops of red food colouring into second part and blend 30g (1 1/4 oz) grated chocolate into last part. Arrange these 3 parts of dough into triangles next to each other into second cake form, which was also greased and floured. Bake. Dice cooled colored dough. Slice first half of baked dough into 2 layers and spread with jelly. Place bottom half into cake form lined with wax paper. Prepare punch mixture. Boil water with sugar, add jelly and boil for 2 minutes. Cool. Add juice of 1 lemon and 1 orange, rum and white wine. Soak colored dices in punch mixture and place alternatively on bottom part of cake, covering it completely. Pour in remaining punch and cover with second layer of cake, spread with jelly. Place cake upside down on board, weigh down and leave until next day. Remove cake form and spread with punch frosting.

Walnut Cake

DOUGH: 5 eggs, 100 g (4 oz) powder sugar, 1/2 vanilla bean, 250 g (8 oz) ground walnuts, 2 Tbsp. grated biscuits.

CREAM: 1/2 l (1 pint) milk, 1 vanilla pudding (custard powder), 3 Tbsp. sugar, 250 g (8 oz) soft butter, 100 g (4 oz) powder sugar, 2 egg yolks, 100 g (4 oz) coarsely chopped walnuts.

Beat egg yolks with sugar and scraped inside of vanilla bean. Fold in stiff beaten egg whites. Gradually mix in ground walnuts and grated biscuits. Place dough into buttered and floured cake form, bake in preheated oven for 30–35 minutes. Cook cream using milk, pudding powder and sugar, cool. Cream soft butter with sugar until smooth, gradually adding 2 egg yolks. Then slowly add cream, mix well. Slice cake twice into layers, spread the top and sides of cake with cream and sprinkle with nuts.

Linz Cake

280 g (10 oz) flour, 240 g (8 oz) soft butter, 200 g (8 oz) powder sugar, 100 g (4 oz) blanched ground almonds, 2 eggs, 2 egg yolks, 1 tsp. baking powder, grated lemon rind from 1/4 lemon, vanilla sugar, 1 egg for brushing, 120 g (5 oz) raspberry jelly.

Mix together flour, butter, sugar, almonds, lemon rind, vanilla sugar, eggs, egg yolks and baking powder, using electric mixer, then work dough with hands. Wrap dough in foil and leave for 3 hours in refrigerator. Roll out 2/3 of dough between two foils, spread with raspberry jelly. Roll out remaining dough sprinkled with flour, again between foil. Slice into strips about 1 inch wide and place on cake to form lattice. Brush strips with beaten egg, bake 25–30 minutes.

Rhubarb Tart

1 kg (2 lbs) rhubarb, 250 g (8 oz) butter, 250 g (8 oz) sugar, 1 vanilla sugar, pinch of salt, 4 eggs, 300 g (11 oz) flour, 100 g (4 oz) potato flour, 1 pkg. baking powder, grated rind of 1 lemon, 100 g (4 oz) ground almonds.

Clean rhubarb and chop into about 1 inch pieces. Mix butter, sugar, vanilla sugar and salt. Gradually add eggs, flour, potato flour, baking powder, lemon rind and almonds. Add rhubarb last. Spread dough on greased baking sheet and bake in preheated oven for about 50 minutes.

One Meter Tart

DOUGH: 4 eggs, 250 g (8 oz) sugar, 260 g (8 1/4 oz) flour, 10 Tbsp. oil, 8 Tbsp. warm water, 1/2 pkg. baking powder, 1 tsp. cocoa.

CREAM: 250 g (8 oz) butter, 1/2 l (1 pint) milk, 1 vanilla pudding powder, 1 vanilla sugar, 100 g (4 oz) powder sugar, 2 Tbsp. rum, chocolate icing and almond for decoration.

Cream egg yolks with sugar. Gradually add oil, water, flour and baking powder. Fold in stiffly beaten egg whites (2). Divide dough in half. Leave one half light, add cocoa to

Fancy Desserts, Cakes and Holiday Treats

second half. Grease and flour two fluted loaf pans (saddle shape), pour in batter, light in one, dark in the other form. Bake. Cool and wrap both pieces in foil. Next day prepare cream using milk, vanilla sugar and pudding powder, boil together. Cool. Cream soft butter with sugar. Add pudding cream and rum to taste, mix well. Slice both "Saddle" loaves thinly. Alternate join with cream one dark and one light slice until all slices form one long cake, about 1 meter (about 1 yard). Spread top with remaining cream, chocolate icing and decorate with almonds. Chill and cut slanting slices with a sharp knife.

"Drunken Frank" – "Opily Frantisek"

DOUGH: 6 eggs, 220 g (8 oz) sugar, 220 g (8 oz) butter, 120 g (5 oz) all purpose flour, 2 tsp. cocoa, 3/4 pkg. baking powder.

FILLING: 250 g (8 oz) ground walnuts, 140 g (6 oz) sugar, 1/2 pkg. vanilla pudding powder, 50 g (2 oz) powder sugar, chocolate icing, red currant jelly.

Beat soft butter, egg yolks and sugar until foamy. Add flour, baking powder and cocoa. Fold in stiffly beaten 2 egg whites. Spread dough on greased baking sheets and bake in preheated oven for 50 minutes. To make filling mix nuts, sugar and rum. To make cream, cook pudding, cool. Cream soft butter with sugar, beat in cooled pudding. Spread baked tart with jelly and nut filling. Spread top with cream and pour on icing. Slice when cool.

Vanilla Crescents

150 g (6 oz) flour, 20 g (3/4 oz) sugar, 50 g (2 oz) ground peeled almonds, 1 vanilla sugar, 1 tsp. grated lemon rind, 110 g (4 1/2 oz) soft butter, 1 egg yolk, 50 g (2 oz) powder sugar, 2 vanilla sugars.

Work flour, sugar, almonds, 1 vanilla sugar, lemon rind, butter and egg yolk into dough. Chill for 1 hour. Form roll with hands, cut into small pieces. Form each piece into a small crescent. Bake on greased baking sheet until golden. While still warm roll in powder sugar mixed with 2 packets of vanilla sugar.

Bear Paws

350 g (12 oz) flour, 200 g (8 oz) ground almonds, 250 g (8 oz) soft butter, 250 g (8 oz) sugar, ground rind of 1/2 lemon, pinch of cinnamon and cloves, 1 egg, 30 g (1 1/4 oz) cocoa.

Mix together flour, sugar, almonds, butter, lemon rind, cinnamon, ground cloves and cocoa. Work into dough. Break off small pieces and press into greased and floured bear paw molds. Bake for 20 minutes in a pre-heated 350 °F oven. Cool.

Mouse Horns

75 g (3 oz) butter, 1 Tbsp. whipping cream, 150 g (6 oz) flour, pinch of baking powder, 2 egg whites, 120 g (5 oz) powder sugar, 80 g (3 oz) ground almonds.

Work soft butter, whipping cream, flour and baking powder into dough. Wrap in foil and chill for 1 hour. Roll out dough on floured pastry board very thin and slice into triangles about 5 cm (2 1/2 inches) long. Place on greased baking sheet and pre-bake for 8 minutes. Meanwhile beat 2 egg whites until stiff. Fold in sugar and almonds. Spread this mixture on pre-baked triangles. Bake for 10 more minutes. Cool.

Linz Tarts

250 g (8 oz) soft butter, 20 g (5 oz) sugar, 1 tsp. grated lemon rind, vanilla sugar, 4 egg yolks, 350 g (12 oz) flour, 150 g (6 oz) raspberry or red currant jelly, 50 g (2 oz) powder sugar, 2 vanilla sugars.

Sift flour onto pastry board, place sugar, vanilla sugar, lemon rind and egg yolks in the middle. Mix dough well and place in refrigerator for 2 hours. Then roll out about 1/4 inch thick. Cut out circles, in half of the circles cut out smaller circles in the center. Place on an ungreased baking sheet and bake for 10–15 minutes. When cool spread whole cookies with jelly and place the cookies with holes on top and sprinkle with powder sugar.

Fancy Desserts, Cakes and Holiday Treats

Orange Sticks

125 g (5 oz) butter, 100 g (4 oz) powder sugar, 100 g (4 oz) marzipan (almond paste), 1 egg, 1 orange, 150 g (6 oz) flour, 100 g (4 oz) potato flour, 100 g (4 oz) orange marmalade, 100 g (4 oz) cocoa icing.

Mix soft butter, sugar, crumbled almond paste, egg and grated orange peel. Add flour and potato flour, mix well. Fill pastry bag with dough and squeeze onto greased baking sheet in shape of sticks, bake for 10 minutes. Cool. Join two sticks with marmalade, dipping one end in cocoa icing.

Rum Balls

100 g (4 oz) butter, 1 egg, 100 g (4 oz) powder sugar, 50 g (2 oz) chopped almonds, 50 g (2 oz) chopped hazelnuts, 150 g (6 oz) biscuit crumbs, 50 g (2 oz) rum raisins, 1 tsp. rum, 50 g (2 oz) ground almonds, cherries soaked in rum, 1 tsp. cocoa.

Mix soft butter with egg and sugar. Add chopped almonds, nuts, rum raisins, biscuit crumbs and cocoa. Add rum to taste. Shape small rounds, wrap a cherry in each. Roll in ground almonds.

Gran's Little Cakes

DOUGH: 210 g (8 oz) flour, 140 g (5 3/4 oz) butter, 70 g (2 1/2 oz) powder sugar, 1 vanilla sugar, grated rind of 1/2 lemon, 140 g (5 3/4 oz) ground blanched almonds, 20 g (3/4 oz) cocoa.

CREAM: 3 egg yolks, 100 g (4 oz) powder sugar, 1 vanilla sugar, 2 Tbsp. red currant or raspberry jelly, 150 g (6 oz) browned ground hazelnuts, 1 Tbsp. rum, biscuit crumbs.

Mix flour, cocoa, sugar, lemon rind and almonds. Add soft butter, work quickly into a dough. Place dough in refrigerator for 1 hour. Roll out into thin sheet, cut out small circles. Bake. Prepare cream. Beat egg yolks with sugar, add jelly, rum and hazelnuts. Add biscuit crumbs as needed. Spread half of circles with cocoa icing, second half with cream. When icing dries, press circles together.